THE ENCYCLOPEDIA OF
WINDOW FASHIONS

For Mary, my heavenly Mother,
Only in your Immaculate arms does my heart find rest.
Mother so sweet, Mother so pure, Mother so kind.
My Mother, My heart

Charles,
Your most unworthy son

Published in the United States by
Charles Randall, Inc.
San Clemente, CA

Distributed in Great Britain by
Antique Collectors Club Ltd
Woodbridge, Suffolk

Sixth United States Edition

Internet: www.randallonline.com

Illustrated by Patricia M. Howard

Cover design by Diego Linares

Interior page design by Chemistry Creative, Minneapolis, MN

Library of Congress Cataloging-in-Publication Data

Randall, Charles T.
  The encyclopedia of window fashions / by Charles T. Randall.-- 6th U.S. ed.
      p. cm.
  Includes bibliographical references and index.
  ISBN 1-890379-12-3 (pbk.)
  1. Draperies in interior decoration. 2. Window shades. I. Title.
  NK2115.5.D73R36 2006
  747'.3--dc22
                                    2005035872

CONTENTS

CONTENTS

INTRODUCTION

WHEN STRIVING FOR SUCCESS, ONE MUST FIRST STRIVE FOR KNOWLEDGE. And, as one begins to learn about that which they desire, one becomes better prepared to obtain it. To help you achieve your own perfect window treatment is the goal of *The Encyclopedia of Window Fashions*.

Is one picture worth a thousand words? Graphics have always stimulated the creation and communication of ideas. The uniqueness—and success—of *The Encyclopedia of Window Fashions* lies in combining the presentation of 2000 illustrations with a truly encyclopedic display of window treatments. Twenty years and one million copies later, this original publication remains the most well-organized, effective design aid available. If your profession is interior design, this newly expanded edition belongs in your library, on your worktable and with you in the field.

Visual definitions of a particular window treatment are immediately effective communication tools. When accompanied by specific yardage requirements, by glossary-supplied performance summaries of fabric properties and appearance by alternative approaches to creating a desired effect, you have all the information necessary to work with your client. Whether a budget is lavish or modest, *The Encyclopedia of Window Fashions* offers the optimum number of choices in an individual design situation.

If this is your introduction to *The Encyclopedia of Window Fashions*, welcome! Our book is sure to become an indispensable resource tool in your work. If you are among the many who own an earlier edition, I extend my sincere appreciation. Without your patronage, our latest version would not be possible. I know you will find that it continues in the high tradition you have come to expect from us.

Charles T. Randall

ABOUT THE ILLUSTRATOR
Patricia Marovich Howard

Art in one form or another has been part of Pat Howard's life as long as she can remember. Her first formal art training came through the Kamas City Art Institute where, upon graduating from high school, she was awarded a scholarship. Completing a year there, she became a full time member of the Hallmark Greeting Card Company design staff where she worked as a card designer for several years. Since all of the original work at Hallmark was done in watercolor, she had plenty of practice.

Moving to Los Angeles to complete her art education, she was accepted at the prestigious Art Center College of Design. After finishing, she began a varied and rewarding career that included work as an illustrator and muralist for a number of Los Angeles design firms, all the time continuing to develop her watercolor skills.

She now owns Design Visuals, a company specializing in interior and architectural illustration and visual presentations for interior designer and architects.

Pat has continued her study of watercolor through classes and workshops with such well known artists as Edward Reep, James Couper Wright, Walter Askin, Richard Yip, Sueo Serisawa, Roger Armstrong, Carolyn Lord and Milford Zornes.

OVERLAPPING STYLES

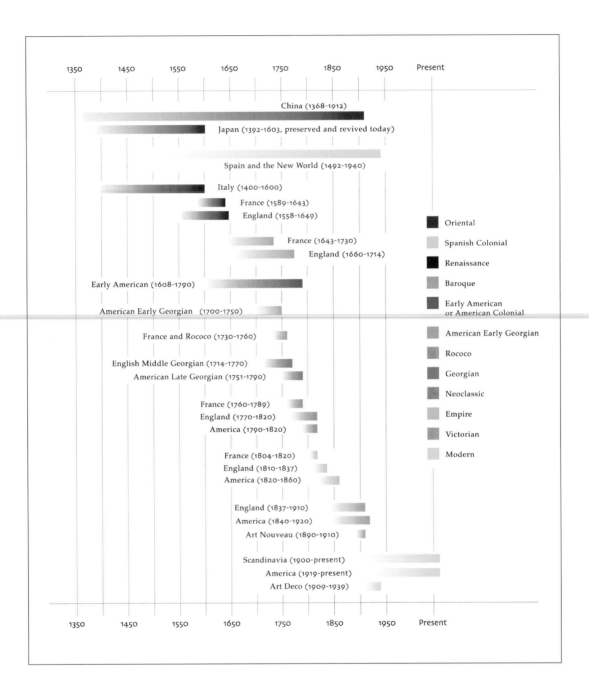

The chart above represents the approximate dates of period styles as they relate to art, architecture and interior design. There was some overlapping of dates as styles changed in various regions at different times. For example, the Renaissance started in Italy but it took many years for the style of that period to reach England and France, by which time the Baroque Era had already begun in Italy.

HISTORICAL WINDOW TREATMENTS

A S TIME MARCHES ON, so does the evolution of window treatments as a means of protection, security and beauty, to name a few. In this chapter, we will explore their ever-changing façades from the years 1440–1901, from the Renaissance through Victorian eras.

THE RECORDED HISTORY OF INTERIOR DECORATION starts with the Renaissance Era. It was during this time of great change and rebirth in the world of art and architecture that interior design became recognized as a specific art form. The concept of intentionally using one's interior furnishings as decoration, integrating fabrics in a unified and harmonious manner, gained popularity throughout Europe. The values and ideas of "civilized life indoors" began to follow a set of established principles. Thus began the art of interior design and the development of the window covering industry.

Wooden shutters were the primary style of window covering used during the Renaissance period. Mounted on either the interior or exterior of the house, shutters could be closed over the window opening to protect

from rain and block out strong sunlight, but did little to provide warmth. Shutters served a purely functional purpose.

The introduction of sheer fabrics allowed for simple, utilitarian curtain making during the sixteenth century. The curtains, most often made of a fine gauze or muslin, provided sun control and some degree of privacy. Hung from iron rods with hooks, usually in single panels, curtains did not become commonplace until after the 1650s.

Although decoration of windows during the Renaissance period was typically simple and understated, bed enclosures and partitions between rooms had curtains that were more elaborate. This allowed for privacy and

prevented drafts and noises from traveling throughout the house. Curtains of this type were called *portiere*, derived from the French word *porte*, meaning door. The portiere would be hung *ensuite* (within the room). A panel of fabric, perhaps in silk, linen or wool, would be tied to one side during the day and pulled over the door at night for privacy.

During this era, this bed was a person's most cherished possession. Bedrooms of the nobility needed to reflect the importance of their owners. Four-poster beds with canopies were large wooden structures with elaborate hand-carved motifs. Bed hangings were mounted under the canopies to close off the bed. In northern climates, this was to provide warmth and prevent drafts, whereas in the warmer Mediterranean countries,

the primary function was to protect from insects. In fact, the word canopy is believed to be derived from the Greek word *konops*, meaning gnat.

Fabrics at this time were mostly plain weaves of silk, wool or cotton. As new weaving methods were developed, velvets and brocades in rich and vibrant colors became widely used throughout France and Italy. Cotton fabrics now had hand-blocked prints and painted designs in large floral patterns.

Toward the end of the Renaissance, valances began to be incorporated into window treatments. Swags and pelmets, inspired by classical Greek motifs, became the finishing touches to a more elaborate look that flourished during the Baroque era.

THE BAROQUE PERIOD MARKED GREAT DEVELOPMENTS in window dressing. For the first time in history, window curtains became a deliberate and distinctive decorative element to the interior design of a room. New advances in weaving techniques, coupled with increased imports of cotton textiles from India, created new fabrics specifically for use in curtaining.

"More elaborate" and "theatrical" are the most common descriptions of all window coverings of the Baroque era. Cornices and pelmuts gained importance as the preferred method of finishing the top of a window treatment, their primary function being to conceal the rods and workings of the curtains mounted beneath. Cornices were made of wood and usually hand-carved in very intricate patterns. A pelmut differs

from a cornice in that it is usually made of stiffened fabric, shaped and often embellished with hand-made, decorative edgings.

Passementerie, the art of making decorative trims, flourished during the reign of Louis XIV in France. Later the Huguenots, facing religious persecution, fled to Germany, England and the Netherlands, taking with them the skills of their intricate crafts.

The beautiful trimmings initially used to disguise the seams and joins on draperies evolved into decorative details reserved for royalty and nobility. Flat braids, tasseled fringes and soutache made of fine silk yarns adorned the edges of velvets, brocades and damasks during the height of the Baroque era.

Window curtains had previously been simple, single panels of fabric. The innovation of designing them in pairs created symmetry at the window. These sets of curtains were usually tied back with a piece of fabric or a metal holdback during the day and drawn across the window for privacy at night.

Daniel Marot, a French artist and upholsterer of the seventeenth century, is credited with designing the festoon, a drapery that can be pulled up on the window, creating a swagged effect. From this concept, many varied styles of blinds and valances developed, of which the swag and tail are most notable.

Sashes provided sun control on windows during the day. These were made of very fine, sheer fabric, stretched onto a frame and soaked in oil. The frame was mounted against the window and the oil soaked

fabric became translucent, providing a sun barrier.

Bed canopies also became more elaborate. The actual wood structure was smaller than during the Renaissance, but the bed hangings and curtains reached new levels of opulence and detailing. Rich embroidered tapestries and silks often were draped from rods mounted under the wood structure.

Early Georgian was the decorative style of England and America during the Baroque period in Europe. While the Early Georgian look was greatly influenced by the French Baroque, it was implemented in a more refined way. Many of the designs that define early Georgian are attributed to Sir Christopher Wren, the Royal Architect of England during the late 1600s.

THE MOST SIGNIFICANT CONCEPT THAT DEVELOPED during the Late Georgian period was the idea of matching window curtains and bed hangings. Previously, these two elements were regarded as unrelated in the interior design of a room. Rich damasks and brocades in gold, blue and red hues were now used for both draperies and bed enclosures. Other colors that dominated interior design during this era included turquoise, teal and coral.

Bed hangings were commonplace throughout Europe by this time, providing warmth and decoration to the stately rooms of the era. Cotton chintz fabrics, block printed in English garden patterns, were more affordable for the middle class of this time, and increased the popularity of these furnishings. Households of the

wealthy would have two sets of bed hangings, a heavy tapestry fabric for winter months and lighter muslin fabric for summer.

Elegantly shaped and elaborately embellished pelmets dominated the silhouette of the Late Georgian period. Appliqué and embroidery techniques further enriched the look of the designs. Billowing festoon blinds, which were pulled up under the pelmets by means of cords, were regarded as the most fashionable look in Europe.

Window treatments during the Late Georgian Era could be described as more fluid. The newest fabrics and designs had a soft flow not previously achieved in window coverings. Adding to this feeling of movement was

the use of ribbons and garlands as motifs on patterned fabrics.

Italian stringing, or reefed curtains, were more popular during this time in England. These drapery panels were made to create a festooned look by pulling a string diagonally toward the upper outside corners of the window, causing the curtain fabric to billow and swag gracefully. Interior designers today still use this very elegant method of creating a festoon.

The oil soaked sashes of the Baroque era were still in common use as a means of sun control during this time. Often hand-painted with intricate designs or outdoor scenes, the sashes became the precursor to roller shades, which were introduced toward the end of this period. Roller blinds were made of natural linen or cotton and used a pulley system to be raised or lowered for sun control and privacy.

Window coverings were becoming more complex as architects began designing window styles and shapes based on the proportions established by sixteenth century Italian architect Andrea Palladio's ideals, called the Palladian principles. These were a specific set of proportions based on the classical architecture of ancient Greece that could be applied to various exterior elements, including windows.

UPHOLSTERERS FROM THE BAROQUE THROUGH THE VICTORIAN ERAS were solely responsible for the interior design of a home. The finely-made bed hangings and window treatments were the designs of these skilled and influential men. They dutifully commissioned and supervised the various trades required to execute their lavish designs. One such man was Thomas Chippendale.

In 1754, Chippendale published a greatly influential pattern book of designs, *The Gentleman and Cabinet-Makers Director*. Chippendale commonly used motifs of Chinese influence as well as the trademark shell design of the Rococo period. These motifs were used in fabric patterns, as well as the richly-carved wooden structure of beds and other furniture.

Window shapes of this era posed many difficulties, as they often do today. The Gothic-peaked window and Palladian-arch window were common throughout Europe and Britain. Chippendale created curved pelmet boards and lambrequins to decorate these windows and then draped them with softly folded swags.

Much of this era took on a lighter approach to draperies and bed hangings, favoring a greater desire for comfort. Lightweight silk taffeta called *quinze-seize* was the most common fabric for window curtaining and was made in the new lighter hues that typified this period. Colors were more refined; soft pastels in yellow, pink and blue replaced the dark jewel tones of the previous century.

Pull-up curtains, and what were referred to as Roman drapery curtains, were the most fashionable window

coverings of the day. Additional fullness was included in the styling of the pull curtains, giving them a softer look. These curtains were paired with draperies of a richer, darker fabric on top or with an embellished pelmet.

Developments in the textile industry during this era allowed for the creation of fabrics that would take on timeless qualities. *Toiles de Jouy* was a printed fabric from the village of Jouy in France. It literally means the work of Jouy and is the origin of fabric that today is known simply as *toile*. Toile was the first fabric to be printed using the copperplate method. This method produced fabrics that had better definition of design and allowed for a larger repeat. Glazing fabrics to produce *chintz* was also introduced during this time.

The wooden structure of the bed was redefined in several variations as canopies adopted a lighter look. The *half tester* was a shorter canopy that projected out from the wall over a portion of the bed rather than the whole length. *Lit a la polonaise* was a domed canopy supported by rods on each of the four corners and disguised by beautiful silk panels. In France, it had become common to place beds in alcoves and build lambrequins graced with side panels around them.

Cotton and silk replaced heavier fabrics such as velvet and tapestry used for the canopies and bed hangings during the Baroque era. The Rococo period marked a transition from the very ornate, elaborate style in the Baroque Era to a refined and classic style that dominated the neoclassic period of the late eighteenth century.

NEOCLASSICISM IS AN ELEGANT STYLE OF DESIGN characterized by simple, geometric forms. Ancient Greek and Roman Classical artifacts, found in the excavations at Pompeii and Herculaneum during the 1700s, inspired this styling.

Discoveries at these ruins also inspired popular colors during the Neoclassic Era. A palette of earth tones including clay, terracotta and green were all accented with black. Other influences for decorative colors came from industry rather than history. Wedgwood pottery inspired a range of blue colors that was popular at this time, and the colors used in the tapestry factories Aubusson and Gobelins in France also contributed to the color trends.

The designing of beds and bed canopies became the responsibility of the cabinetmaker rather than the upholsterer at this time. This resulted in less focus on the bed hangings as well as the introduction of coordinated cornices for both the bed and window. One cabinetmaker whose designs were influential in the late 1700s was Thomas Sheraton.

Sheraton was renowned for unique beds and elaborate cornices. The introduction of the Pagoda cornice, with a distinctly Chinese influence, is credited to Sheraton. His designs, published in the 1793 pattern book *Cabinet-maker and Upholsterer's Drawing Book*, were carved and gilded with Classical motifs.

Draperies, made in pairs for symmetry, were the most common style of window covering in the Neoclassic

Era. This simpler look led to the need to improve the rods used for decorative purposes or functionality. The introduction at this time of the first cord and pulley style rod, now known as a traverse rod, reduced wear and tear on draperies.

These new rods had an overlap in the center that greatly enhanced the finished look of the draperies. In addition, decorative rods with elaborate finials and rings gave interest and balance to the simplicity of the silhouette of this time.

Layers of curtains were added beneath the over drapes as sheers gained popularity. These muslin curtains were installed onto the window frame to provide added privacy and sun protection in a room.

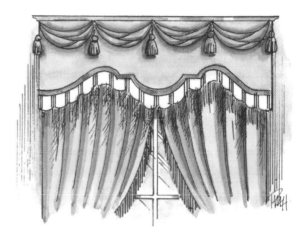

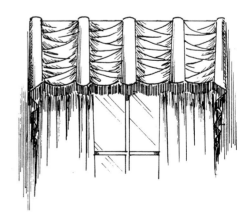

    The biggest technological achievement in the production of decorative textiles in this era was the invention of the Jacquard loom by Joseph Jacquard in 1804. This complex loom allowed the most intricate patterns to be woven into fabric by machine, something that could only be done painstakingly, by hand, in the past.

    Toward the end of the Neoclassic period, the sharp symmetry that silhouetted the drapery styling was replaced by an asymmetrical look that was later popularized in the Empire period.

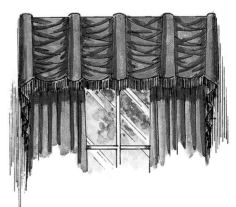

ONCE HEALTH CONCERNS AROSE THAT BED HANGINGS AND CANOPIES reduced air circulation and attracted dust, and that wooden structures housed insects, open beds made of iron replaced them. This resulted in a greater emphasis on bed coverings and window treatments during the Empire and Regency Periods.

With the same concerns that saw the demise of the canopy bed, pelmets and cornices also became less important. Window treatments maintained a look of opulence as multiple layers of curtains were now used, often in an asymmetrical styling. It was not uncommon for a window to have four or five individual layers of curtains—an over drape, an under curtain made of a lighter-weight fabric, a sub curtain and blinds, and

possibly a swag valance mounted over the entire ensemble.

The popularity of the sheer sub curtain continued to rise during the Empire period. Made of silk or cotton muslin, these became standard window coverings in neutral hues. Alternatively, glass curtains, also made of muslin, were used in less formal room settings and fitted on the lower half of the window, next to the panes of glass. History suggests that both types of curtain served to protect against unwanted insects entering through open windows and to filter the light from the sun.

The elimination of pelmets and cornices necessitated in refining and designing more intricate drapery headings and rods. French pleats, goblet pleats and smocked headings maintained folds in a more regulated and

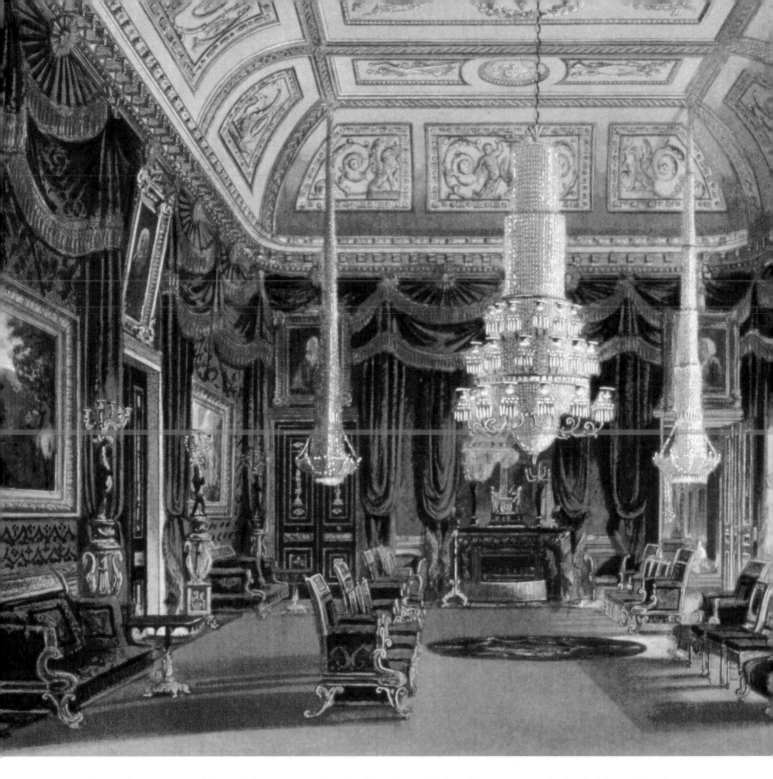

decorative manner while rods became opulent display pieces. Made of brass or wood, the finials and brackets of these rods took inspiration from classic motifs such as laurel and acanthus leafs, and military ornamentation such as spearheads and eagles.

"Continued drapery", a term used to describe the practice of disguising two or more separate windows as one by means of a continuous valance or rod, easily lent itself to the asymmetrical designs of this era. Each window alone was asymmetrical, but when coupled with the other windows within the arrangement, the mirror image would create a balanced effect.

The popularity of the puddled drapery increased during the Empire period. Designers of the time differed

in opinion as to what length was appropriate, from a few inches hanging gracefully on the floor to yards of fabric creating a more dramatic, puddled effect.

Historians also differ in opinion as to the reason for the extra length of fabrics used in what some termed, receptacles for dust. Some believe that the length of draperies represented wealth: the more fabric that a person could afford, the wealthier that they were. Others believe that it was purely functional: to stop drafts from the window. This is especially likely since the bed hangings of previous times had been eliminated.

Another decorative detail widely used throughout this time was reverse lining. A secondary fabric could give the effect of an additional layer of drapery, when used as the lining of the main drapery, which was turned

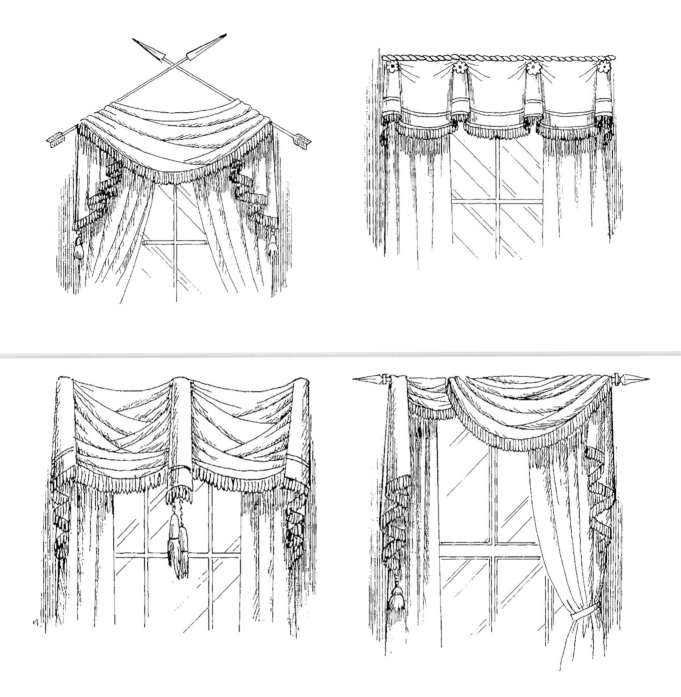

back or reversed to reveal the contrast fabric.

Roller blinds added an artistic element to interior design. These became the canvases for landscape paintings and printed designs. Sometimes trimmed with fringe or borders, roller blinds were often an integral part of a window treatment during this period.

Historically, window treatments evolve in cycles of lavishness and opulence to periods of understated simplicity with transitory periods building up to a crescendo. The layered styling of the Empire and Regency periods was the transitory time cresting toward the opulent look of the Victorian Era.

THE VICTORIAN ERA WAS A COMPLEX PERIOD WITH MANY DIFFERENT PHASES defining it. Historians agree, however that it was a time of excessiveness and clutter. The multiple layers of curtaining that dominated the silhouette were a reflection of the extravagant look of the Victorian interior. As in the past, it was not unusual for a window treatment to consist of four or five layers of curtains.

Details using fabrics and fringes were the trend. Bands of contrast fabric were often applied to the edges of draperies and valances. The much heavier look of bouillon fringe replaced tassel fringe and braids.

Lace grew in popularity for use as under curtains and glass curtains. Machine-made laces and netting made these fabrics more affordable to the middle class. Lace or sheer panels were gathered onto brass rods and

The Encyclopedia of Window Fashions

either hung freely at the bottom or attached to the window frame with a second rod at the hem. When used in bedrooms or on doors, these panels would be tied with ribbon, pulling in at the center and creating an hourglass effect.

Respected designers of the time advised their clients on the importance of adding lining and interlining to draperies. Not only would the lining extend the life of the fabric, it would provide thermal qualities and help prevent other furnishings from becoming bleached by the sun.

It was the opinion of noted designer John Loudon that draperies could not perform the function of preventing drafts unless a cornice valance was used. This wooden box would close off the space at the top of

the curtains that could allow cold air to circulate. The cornices used during this era were smaller and less ornate than those of earlier periods, though still gilded and sometimes augmented with brass ornamentation.

Lambrequins, an elongated version of the cornice, which exhibited "legs" extending down the sides of a window, had been in vogue during the Empire and early Victorian eras but became obsolete by the end of the nineteenth century. It was felt that these large structures were too heavy for the interiors of the day and blocked out too much light.

New designs in fabric window shades were evolving. More fabric and fullness were constantly being added to create soft billows. The Austrian shade, with smaller, closely-sewn festoons, was the result of this. Swag and

tail valances were often paired with the Austrian curtain for a refined, elegant look.

Roller shades, now manufactured with spring mechanisms, remained an important window covering for privacy and sun control. Other blinds that became highly developed during this time were the wooden horizontal blind and louvered shutters.

Critics of the excessiveness of the Victorian Era started a reform group advocating more simplicity in styling and a return to Gothic design principles. This came to be known as the Aesthetic Movement. William Morris, a name synonymous with decorative fabrics, was a founder of the Aesthetic Movement in interior design. He and other influential designers, such as Charles Eastlake, objected to the suffocating, overly-draped

look of the high Victorian Era. Their designs were kept simple and functional so as to serve only as a background to the room's interior.

The ideals of the Aesthetic Movement prevailed until the end of the nineteenth century when a revival movement reintroduced the French-influenced styling of draperies, returning once again to elaborate cornices, over drapes, under drapes and all the embellishments that typify the window treatments of eras gone by.

DRAPERIES & CURTAINS

WHILE EUROPEANS FIND THE TERMS CURTAINS AND DRAPERIES to be interchangeable, Americans find the pair anything but synonymous. Draperies utilize heavier, lined fabrics, while curtains make use of lighter, sheer materials. It is the curtain that makes full use of breeze entering through an opening window, moving back and forth like breath through the body, playing with the light and offering a delicate touch at the window. Draperies, conversely, are often heavy and substantial enough to block light, provide privacy and beauty, a synergy always welcomed in the home.

Pointed valance with swags over pleated draperies

Pleated draperies with specialty
heading and tassels

Tab draperies with teardrop valance

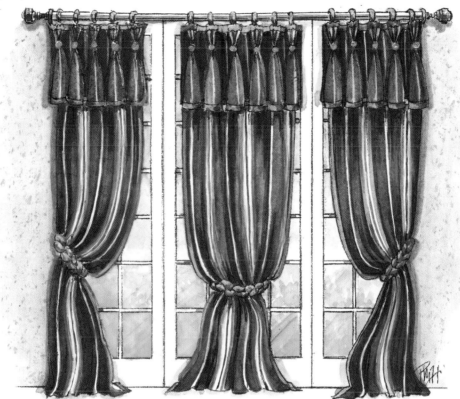

French pleated valance with buttons over tiebacks

Asymmetrical valances over pleated
draperies and Roman shade

Tab valance over draperies

Various rod pocket draperies

Draperies over cloud shade

Arched ruffled sunburst and tiebacks over café curtains

Tent draperies over café curtains

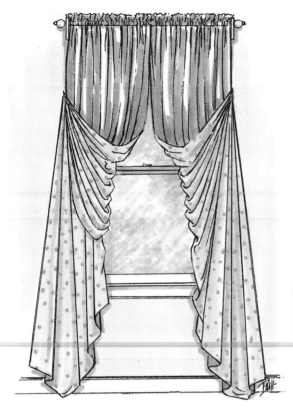

Gathered draperies pulled back to show lining

Tent-pleated draperies over café curtains

Handkerchief valance over asymmetrical tieback

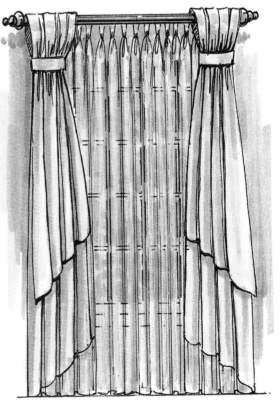

Draperies folded and gathered over sheers

Rod pocket draperies under knotted scarf swag

Gathered draperies over swag

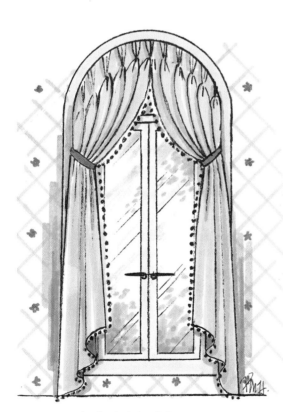

Arched pleated draperies

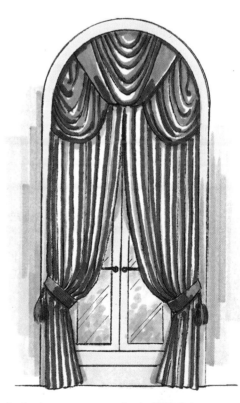

Arched swags over arched pleated draperies

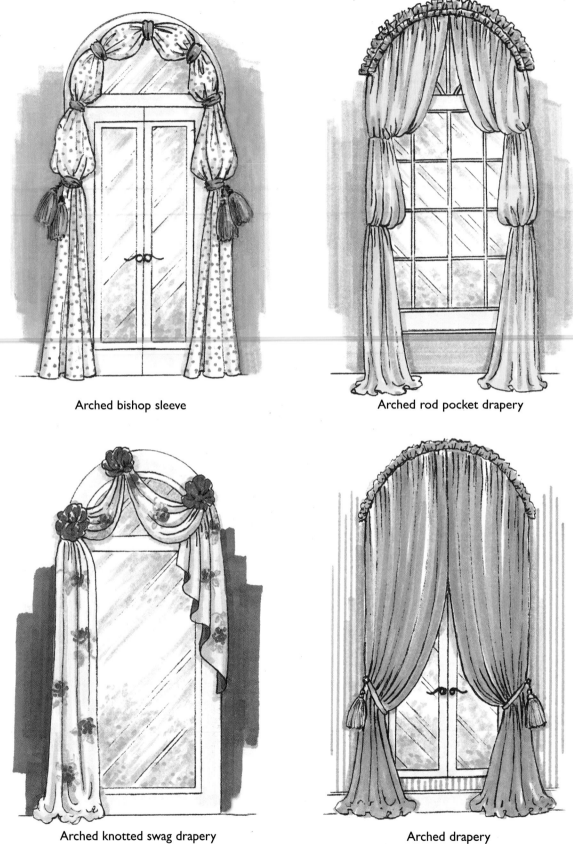

Arched bishop sleeve

Arched rod pocket drapery

Arched knotted swag drapery

Arched drapery

Gathered drapery over Austrian shade

Tab draperies under swag

Arched draperies with ruffles and large ties

Rod pocket draperies with banding

DRAPERY & CURTAIN GALLERY

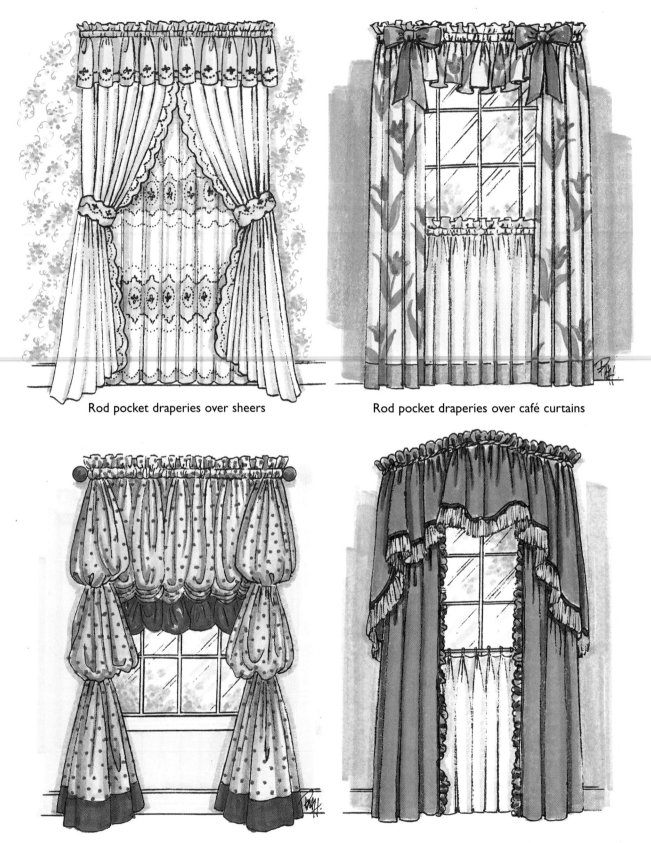

Rod pocket draperies over sheers

Rod pocket draperies over café curtains

Rod pocket bishop sleeve draperies

Arched rod pocket draperies over café curtains

Pleated drapery with tassels and rope

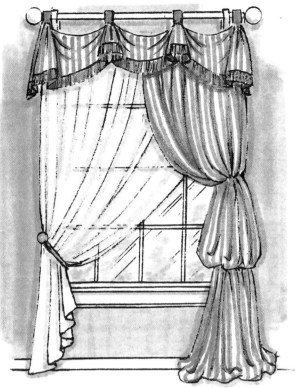

Rod pocket drapery over sheers
with tab valance

Double rod pocket drapery tied back

Tab top draperies layered under scarf swag

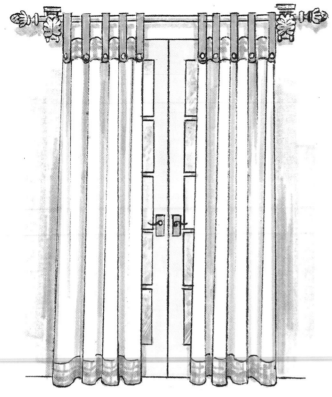

Tab draperies on decorative rod with sconces

Tab drapery on decorative rod with matching holdback

Tab draperies on decorative rod with matching holdbacks

Double tab draperies on decorative rod with matching holdbacks

Arched bishop sleeve draperies
over balloon shade

Knotted lace swag over lace draperies

Arched gathered valance over draperies

Single swag with rosettes over draperies and
horizontal blinds

Tabbed draperies with valance

Gathered draperies with rod pocket sleeve

Draperies with bias swag over Roman shade

Athena draperies over horizontal blind

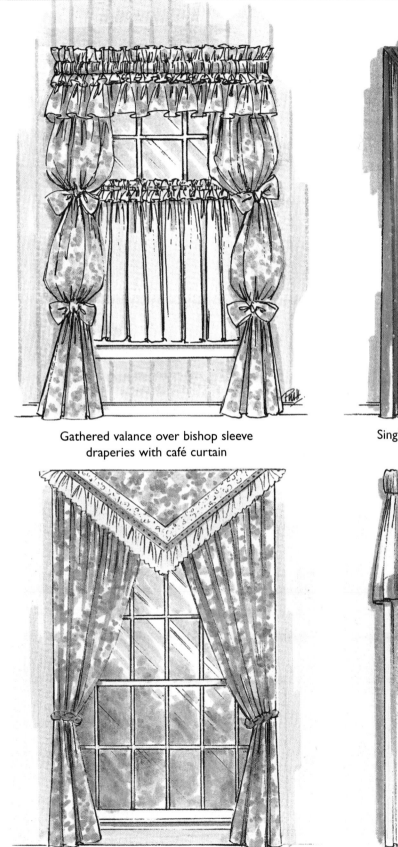

Gathered valance over bishop sleeve
draperies with café curtain

Single swag over draperies and café curtain

Triangle valance over tiebacks

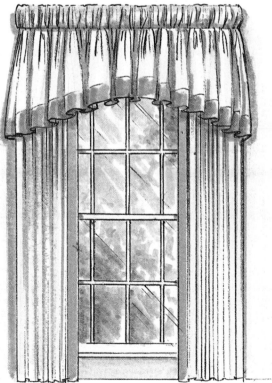

Gathered valance over draperies

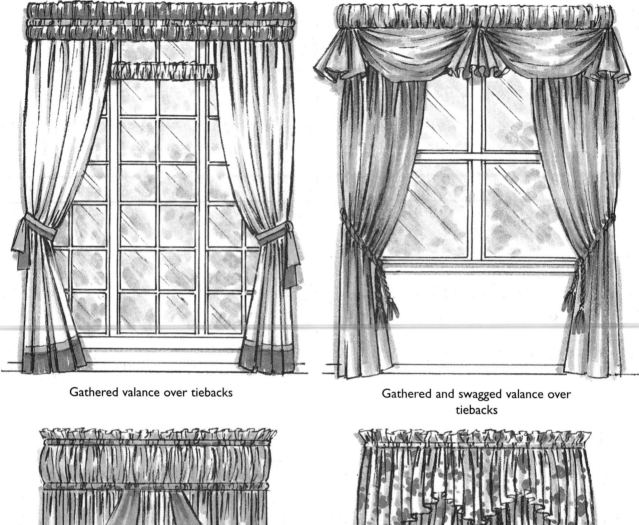

Gathered valance over tiebacks

Gathered and swagged valance over tiebacks

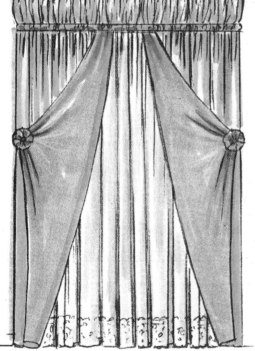

Gathered valance with draperies pulled back over sheers

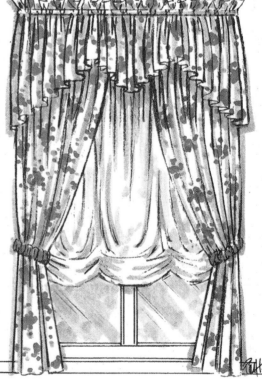

Double arched valance over tiebacks and cloud shade

Pleated arched valance over tiebacks and
sheer balloon shade

Gathered-top arched valance
over bow tiebacks

Double-gathered valance, with brass rod in
middle, over horizontal blind

Tabbed drapery with bows and tieback

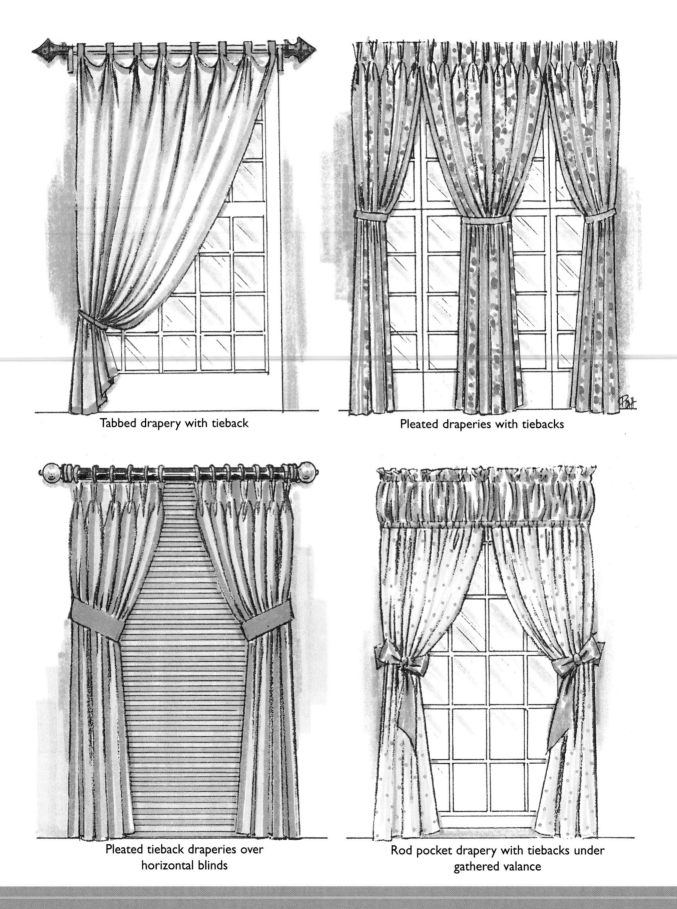

Tabbed drapery with tieback

Pleated draperies with tiebacks

Pleated tieback draperies over
horizontal blinds

Rod pocket drapery with tiebacks under
gathered valance

Rod pocket drapery with center sleeve and tiebacks

Alternate heading styles

Double rod pocket drapery under gathered valance

Bishop sleeve draperies with valance

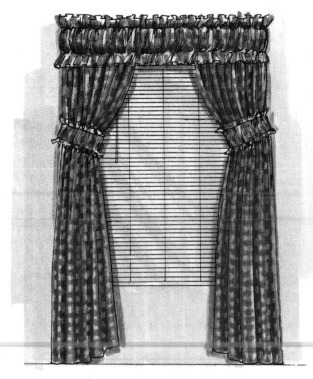

Rod top and bottom valance with matching tiebacks
over mini blind

Flat rod pocket drapery over rod pocket
café curtain

Ruffled rod pocket draperies with tiebacks

Kingston valance over tied-back draperies and sheers

Rod pocket drapery over sheers

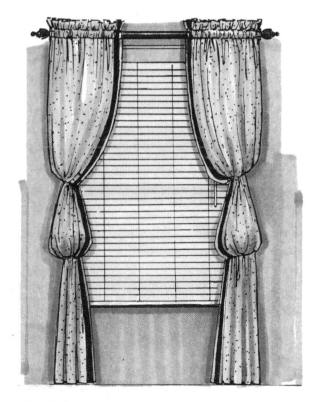

Banded stationary bishop sleeve over mini blinds

Stationary drapery on covered rod with three-inch
stand-up top

Tied-back stationary draperies on decorative rod
with sleeve in middle

Rod top draperies

Bow-tied bishop sleeve draperies gathered
on decorative rod

Stationary rod pocket draperies on
decorative pole with sleeve in middle

Cluster-pleated valance with pleated draperies over Roman shade

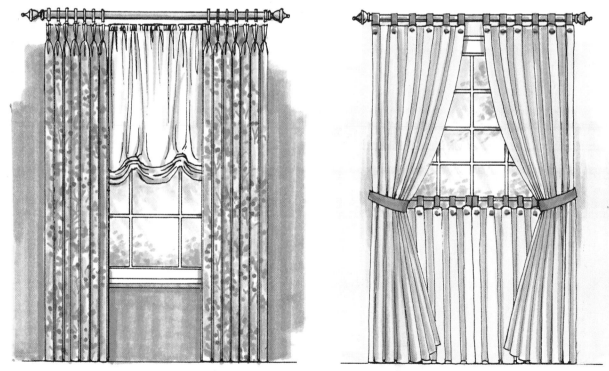

French pleated draperies over balloon shade

Tab draperies over café curtain

Arched French pleated valance and tiebacks

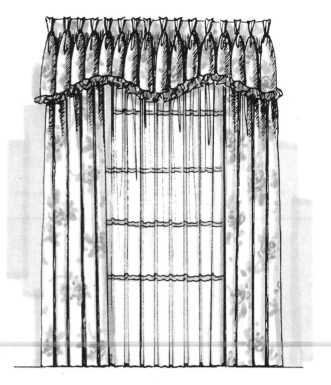

Multiple-arched valance over draperies
and sheers

Rod pocket cloud valance with tiebacks
over sheers

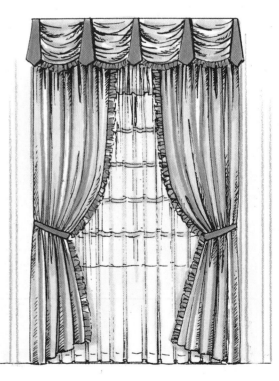

Austrian valance with tiebacks over sheers

Rod pocket draperies with center
Florence and low tiebacks over mini blind

Draperies gathered on decorative rod
over Austrian shade

Rod pocket draperies with multiple bowties over Roman shades

Pleated tieback draperies

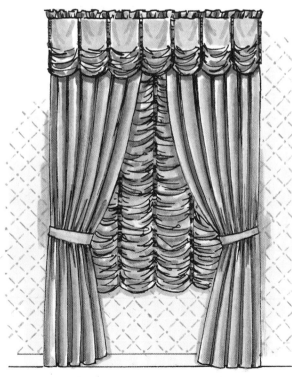

Tieback draperies with balloon valance over
Austrian shade

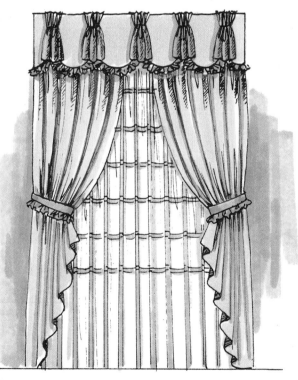

Space pleated Queen Ann valance with
scalloped edge over tiebacks and sheers

Multiple tiebacks over café curtains

Pinch pleated drapery with decorative fringe

Ruffled tiebacks with bow and rosettes over
flat fabric shade

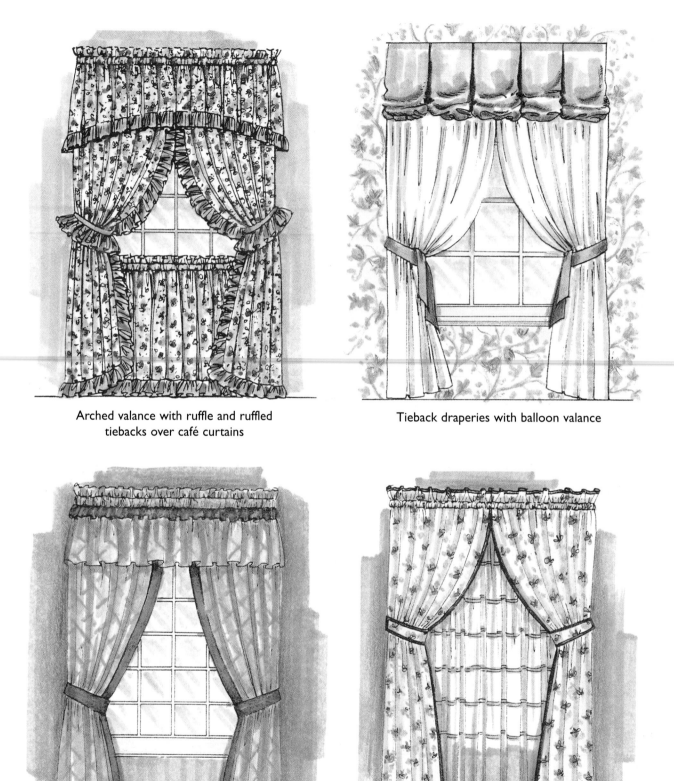

Arched valance with ruffle and ruffled
tiebacks over café curtains

Tieback draperies with balloon valance

Rod pocket drapery with banding

Tiebacks with ruffle at top and sheers under

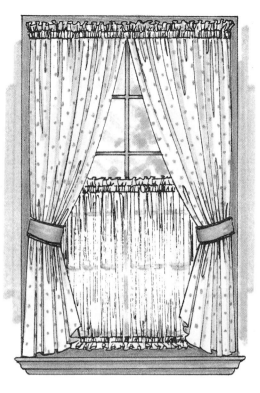

Flat rod pocket drapery, tied back

Rod pocket drapery over café curtain
with rod pocket top and bottom

Rod pocket tiebacks with ruffles

Rod pocket valance with rod pocket café curtains

Tabbed curtain over shutters

Tabbed curtain gathered in the middle

Chevron valance over café curtains

Curtain on decorative rod with holdback

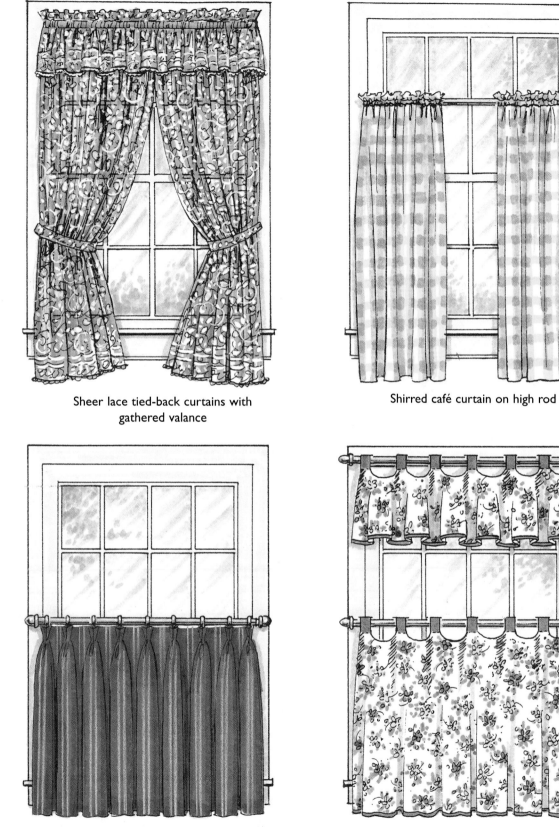

Sheer lace tied-back curtains with
gathered valance

Shirred café curtain on high rod

Café curtain with French pleated tops on rings

Scalloped tab valance over café curtains

Priscilla curtains with ruffles

Valance on brass decorative rod over
tied-back curtains with ruffles

Rod pocket curtains with high ties and large ruffles

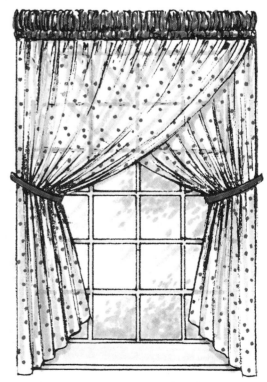

Priscilla curtains with rod pocket top

Café curtains with arched top and valance

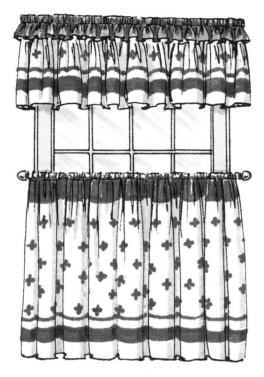

Café curtains on brass rod
with gathered valance

Traditional swag with mini blind

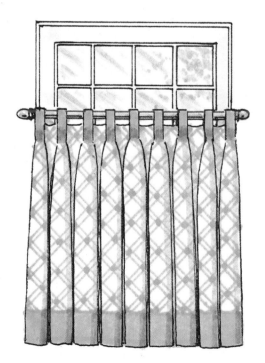

Pleated tab top café curtains on brass rod

Café curtains shirred top-to-bottom
between two rods

Tied-back curtains gathered on a rod

Drapery gathered on a decorative rod
and tied back with large bows

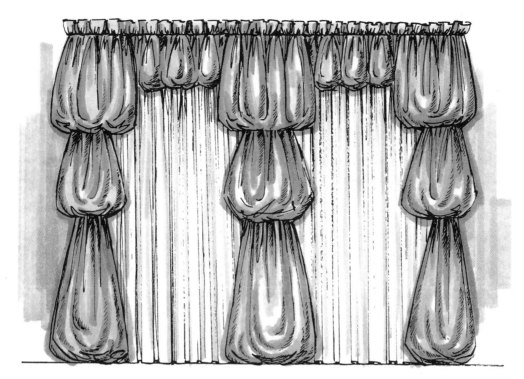

Rod top bishop sleeve draperies over sheers

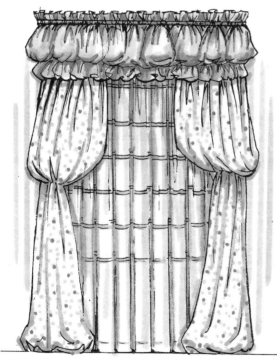

Double rod top valance with puffed tiebacks
over sheers

End-pleated valance with puffed tiebacks
over lace curtains

Bow tied ruffled tiebacks

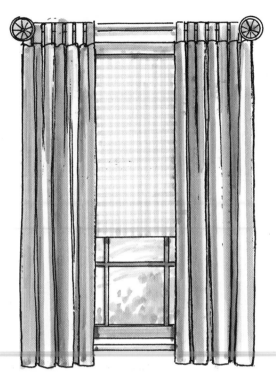

Tab top curtains on decorative rod over
fabric shade

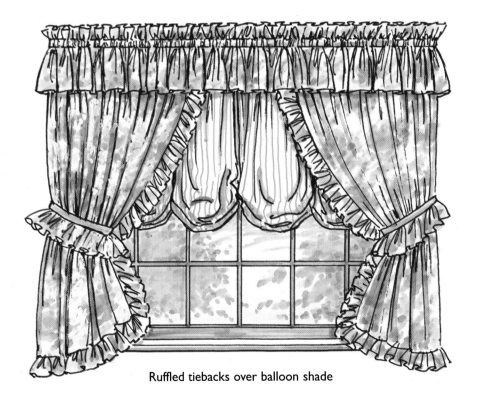

Ruffled tiebacks over balloon shade

Tab top curtains on decorative rod

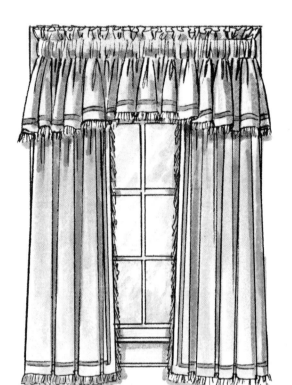

Arched rod pocket valance over straight curtains

Ruffled tiebacks over shutters

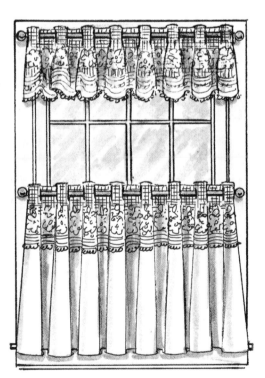

Lace curtains and valance threaded on rod

Banded tieback curtains

Banded valance over tiebacks

Tab top banded curtains tied back

Tiered curtains with ribbon banding

Box pleated with tab heading

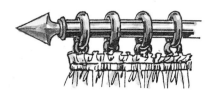

Gathered heading with rings

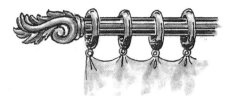

Scalloped heading with sewn-on rings

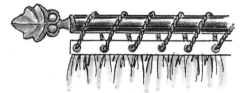

Grommet heading with rope

Scalloped heading with ties

Scalloped and tabbed heading

Tab tied curtains on brass decorative rod

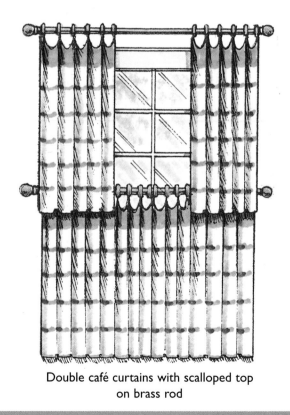

Double café curtains with scalloped top
on brass rod

Specifications

Description:
A window covering topped with decorative pinched folds. Although a simple treatment on its own, it creates a complete look when used under valances or over sheers. It can also be a functional or decorative treatment when used with tiebacks.

Yardage:

<u>Step 1</u>
Width of area to be covered x 2.5 ÷ width of fabric = number of widths (whole numbers only)

<u>Step 2a</u>
Number of widths x (length of window + 16") ÷ 36 = yardage without pattern repeat
—or—

<u>Step 2b</u>
Length + 16" ÷ pattern repeat = number of repeats required (round upward to nearest whole number)

<u>Step 2c</u>
Number of repeats required x pattern repeat = cut length

<u>Step 2d</u>
Number of widths x cut length ÷ 36 = yardage with pattern repeat

Work Order Specifications:
1. Width
2. Length
3. Color of lining
4. Center split, no center split or panel
5. Specify type of rod being used
6. Is treatment going over other treatments?
7. Tiebacks required—see section on tiebacks

Special Note:
A check measure is recommended for all full length drapes.

ATHENA DRAPERIES

Specifications

Description:
This elegant style is created from a flat panel. Rings or brass clips are attached sufficiently apart so as to create a softly swagged effect at the heading when on the rod. The drape often falls gracefully on the floor in a puddle style. A facing of self or contrast fabric is recommended so that the lining will not show at the heading.

Yardage:
Step 1
Width of area to be covered x 2 ÷ width of fabric = number of widths (whole numbers only)
Step 2a
Number of widths x (length + 16") ÷ 36 = yardage without pattern repeat
—or—
Step 2b
Length + 16" ÷ pattern repeat = number of repeats required (round upward to nearest whole number)
Step 2c
Number of repeats required x pattern repeat = cut length
Step 2d
Number of widths x cut length ÷ 36 = yardage with pattern repeat
For self or contrast facing: Allow 1/4 yd. per width

Work Order Specifications:
1. Width of area to be covered
2. Length
3. Color of lining
4. Specify fabric for facing
5. Center split or panel
6. Type of rod, rings being used

Special Note:
1. A puddle of 6" has been allowed in yardage. If more is desired, add to length + allowance.
2. Soft, drapeable fabrics create the best effect.

SHIRRED (SMOCKED) & PENCIL PLEATED DRAPERIES

Description:
An attractive heading that creates even gathers across the width of the drapes. It adds a soft, romantic look to a simple window treatment.

Yardage:

Step 1
  Width of window x 2.5 ÷ width of fabric = number of widths (whole numbers only)

Step 2a
  Number of widths x (length of area to be covered + 16") ÷ 36 = yardage without pattern repeat

—or—

Step 2b
  Length + 16" ÷ pattern repeat = number of repeats required (round upward to nearest whole number)

Step 2c
  Number of repeats required x pattern repeat = cut length

Step 2d
  Number of widths x cut length ÷ 36 = yardage with pattern repeat

Work Order Specifications:
1. Width
2. Length
3. Color of lining
4. Tiebacks required
5. Center split, off center split or panel

Special Note:
1. A check measure is recommended for all full length drapes.
2. Shirred drapes should stay stationary due to the nature of the heading.

Box-pleated Draperies

Description:
A unique alternative to the traditional pinch pleat, box pleats create the very tailored styling of this drape. For optimal effect and function, use either as a stationary treatment with tiebacks or with a decorative rod.

Yardage:
<u>Step 1</u>
Width of area to be covered x 3 ÷ width of fabric = number of widths (whole numbers only)

<u>Step 2a</u>
Number of widths x (length + 16") ÷ 36 = yardage without pattern repeat
—or—

<u>Step 2b</u>
Length + 16" ÷ pattern repeat = number of repeats required (round upward to nearest whole number)

<u>Step 2c</u>
Number of repeats required x pattern repeat = cut length

<u>Step 2d</u>
Number of widths x cut length ÷ 36 = yardage with pattern repeat

Work Order Specifications:
1. Width
2. Length
3. Color of lining
4. Center split, off center split or panel
5. Specify type of rod being used
6. Is treatment going over other treatments?
7. Tiebacks required

Special Note:
1. A check measure is recommended for all full length drapes.
2. Reduce fullness to 2½ if using a traverse rod.

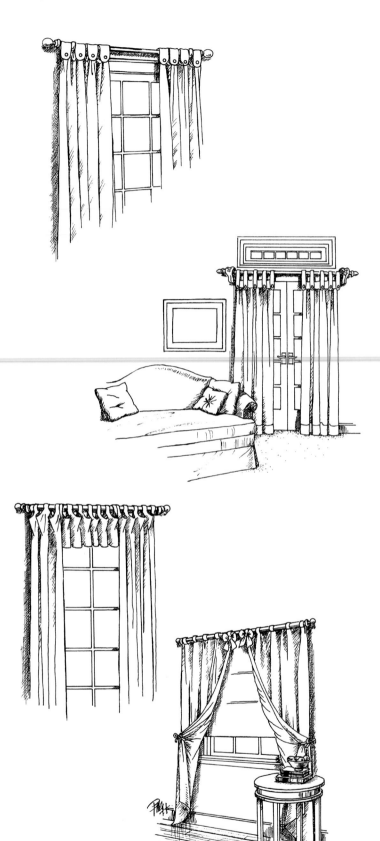

Specifications

Description:
The simple styling of this treatment enhances the beauty of a decorative rod. Fabric loops (tabs) sewn to the top of a flat panel give this treatment a very contemporary look.

Yardage:

Step 1
Width of area to be covered x 1.5 ÷ width of fabric = number of widths (whole numbers only)

Step 2a
Number of widths x (length of area + 24") ÷ 36 = yardage without pattern repeat
—or—

Step 2b
Length + 24" ÷ pattern repeat = number of repeats required (round upward to nearest whole number)

Step 2c
Number of repeats required x pattern repeat = cut length

Step 2d
Number of widths x cut length ÷ 36 = yardage with pattern repeat

Work Order Specifications:
1. Width
2. Length
3. Color of lining
4. Diameter of rod being used

Special Note:
1. Yardage calculations include tabs.
2. Only one and a half times fullness is required on this treatment to obtain the proper effect.

ROD POCKET (SLOTTED) DRAPERIES

Description:

A drapery treatment that creates a shirred heading look by gathering fabric onto a rod. The treatment can be dressed with a ruffle above the rod, or without if being used under a valance. Rod pocket covers can also be used to separate panels.

Yardage:

Step 1
Width of area to be covered x 2.5 ÷ width of fabric = number of widths (whole numbers only)

Step 2a
Number of widths x (length of area + 16") ÷ 36 = yardage without pattern repeat
—or—

Step 2b
Length + 16" ÷ pattern repeat = number of repeats required (round upward to nearest whole number)

Step 2c
Number of repeats required x pattern repeat = cut length

Step 2d
Number of widths x cut length ÷ 36 = yardage with pattern repeat

Work Order Specifications:

1. Width
2. Length
3. Color of lining
4. Size of rod being used
5. Center split or panel
6. Tiebacks required
7. Inside or outside mount
8. Frill size on top of rod (if applicable)

Special Note:

1. This is a stationary treatment.
2. This treatment cannot be used when treatment underneath is mounted up to the ceiling.
3. Extra yardage has to be calculated for rod covers.

TUXEDO (PULL-BACK) DRAPERIES

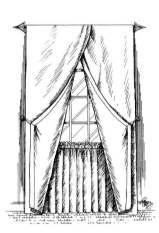

Description:

A contemporary version of a traditional look that consists of a flat or pleated panel simply folded back and tied to reveal the contrast lining.

Yardage (For Flat Panels Only):

Step 1

Width of area being covered + return + 5" ÷ width of fabric = number of widths (whole numbers only)

Step 2a

Number of widths x (length of area + 10") ÷ 36 = yardage without pattern repeat

—or—

Step 2b

Length + 10" ÷ pattern repeat = number of repeats required (round upward to nearest whole number)

Step 2c

Number of repeats required x pattern repeat = cut length

Step 2d

Number of widths x cut length ÷ 36 = yardage with pattern repeat

Step 3

Calculate with same formula for contrast lining

Step 4

Allow 1/2 yard for ties, 1 yard for larger sash ties

Work Order Specifications:

1. Width
2. Length
3. Inside or outside mount
4. Size of returns needed
5. Specify which fabric is to be used as contrast

Special Note:

1. Large returns are not recommended for this treatment.
2. Tuxedo drapes limit the amount of light into a room.
3. Not recommended for windows that are proportionately wider than longer.

Specifications

Description:
A drapery treatment where a 2½" or 4½" shirred heading look is created by gathering fabric onto a flat rod. Two flat rods can be used to create a deeper heading look.

Yardage:
Step 1
Width of area to be covered + 10" x 2.5 ÷ width of fabric = number of widths (whole numbers only)

Step 2a
Number of widths x (length + 20") ÷ 36 = yardage without pattern repeat
—or—

Step 2b
Length + 20" ÷ pattern repeat = number of repeats required (round upward to nearest whole number)

Step 2c
Number of repeats required x pattern repeat = cut length

Step 2d
Number of widths x pattern repeat ÷ 36 = yardage with pattern repeats

Work Order Specifications:
1. Width
2. Length
3. Color of lining
4. Size of rod needed or being used
5. Center split or no center split
6. Tiebacks required
7. Number of tunnels

Special Note:
This is a stationary treatment that will require tiebacks or a rod cover to separate panels.

Specifications

Description:
A drape where the fabric is stretched between two rods creating an all-over shirred effect. An excellent treatment if privacy is required or if working with a narrower window. Add a collar tieback to create a decorative hourglass shape.

Yardage:
Step 1
Width of area to be covered x 2.5 ÷ width of fabric = number of widths
Step 2a
Number of widths x (length of area + 16") ÷ 36 = yardage without pattern repeat
—or—
Step 2b
Length + 16" ÷ pattern repeat = number of repeats required (round upward to nearest whole number)
Step 2c
Number of repeats required x pattern repeat = cut length
Step 2d
Number of widths x cut length ÷ 36 = yardage with pattern repeat

Work Order Specifications:
1. Width
2. Length
3. Color of lining
4. Size of rods being used
5. Inside or outside mounts
6. Frill size top and bottom of rod

Special Note:
1. Stationary treatment.
2. Not recommended for windows larger than 48".
3. A frill is recommended for this treatment to conceal hardware.

Standard Workmanship & Quality Features

- Double heading
- 4" permanent Buckram headings
- Pleating custom tacked with extra thread
- All seams serged and overlocked
- All draperies perfectly matched
- All draperies table sized
- Blind stitched bottom and side hems
- Double 4" bottom hems + 1½" double side hems
- All draperies weighted at corners and seams
- Multiple width draperies are placed so that joining seams are hidden behind pleats

Made to Custom Measurements

- Made to exact width or length
- Pleated to any desired fullness up to 3 to 1, lined or unlined.

Drapery Terminology

- *Width* is one strip of material of any length that can be pleated to a finished dimension across the TOP of between 16" and 24". For example, using a 48" wide material, a width that finishes to 24" is considered double fullness, or 2 to 1; a 16" finished width is considered triple fullness, or 3 to 1. Any number of widths can be joined together so as to properly cover the window area.
- *Panel* is a single drapery unit of one or more widths which is used specifically for one way draw stack left or stack right and/or stationary units.
- *Pair* is two equal panels that cover a desired area.
- *Return* is the measurement from the rod to the wall; in other words, the projection.
- *Overlap* is the measurement, when draperies are fully closed, of the right panel overlapping the left panel. This is usually 3" for each panel. *Remember you must add 12″ to the rod measurement to ensure proper returns and overlaps.*

Options Available on Draperies

A variety of headings:
- Pinch pleated with 4" or 5" buckram
- Box pleated
- Box pleated with tabs for rod. Add diameter of rod to finished length. For flat tab draperies use 2 to 1.
- Rod pocket for shirred draperies
- Self-lined
- Lined with black-out lining

Pleat Spacing

Pleat spacings vary according to the widths of material used to achieve a specified finished width. For example: three widths of material pleated to 59" to the pair will not have the same pleat spacing as three widths of material pleated to 72" to the pair. If pleats and pleat spacing are to look alike on draperies of different widths, you should specify "comparable fullness" when you place an order. *Vertically striped fabrics will not fabricate to allow an identical stripe to fall between each pleat, panel to panel, or pair to pair.*

How to Order Custom-Made Draperies

Since "Made-to-Measure" draperies are made to your exact specifications, it is imperative that measurements be made with the greatest care. We recommend that you double-check all measurements for accuracy. All measuring should be done with a steel tape or yardstick. Measure each window separately even when they appear to be the same size. If length varies, use the dimension of shortest length.

Drapery Width

- Measure width of drapery rod from end to end.
- Add to this figure an extra 12" to include the allowance for standard traverse rod returns and overlap.
- Standard returns are 3" in depth. For over-draperies allow for clearance of under-curtain. A 6" return is usually sufficient.
- When ordering panels that stack (draw) in one direction only, specify whether the drapery is to stack to the left or right.

Drapery Length

- Measure from top of rod, to floor, to carpet. (By inserting pins 1" from top, drapery will automatically clear the floor or carpet.)
- Undercurtain should be at least ½" shorter than over-drapery.
- When floor-length draperies are used, it is best to measure length at each side and in the center. Use the shortest figure for your measurements.
- Rod should be placed a minimum of 4" above the window so that hooks and pleats will not be observed from the outside.
- If sill-length, allow 4" below sill so that the bottom hem will not be observed from the outside.
- When using pole rings, measure lengths from bottom of rings.

Caution: When both under-curtain and over-drapery are used, be sure to allow for clearance of face drapery. For example, an under-curtain with a 3½″ return requires at least a 6″ return on the over-drapery.

CALCULATING YARDAGES

WITH DRAPERY CALCULATIONS, ONE MUST CONSIDER the following: width and length of window or area to be covered, amount of fullness desired, width of fabric to be used, allowances for hems, headings and styling and pattern repeat, if applicable. And after obtaining accurate measurements for each, proceed with the following steps.

Step 1) Determine the number of fabric widths required. This is calculated by multiplying the width of the window or area to be covered by the given fullness factor (listed on the item page). Divide this by the width of the fabric being used. The result is the number of widths of fabric that are required to achieve the desired fullness. Since fabric suppliers will not sell a part of the width, this figure must be a whole number.

Step 2a) Calculate the yardage. Add to the length of the window, or area to be covered, the allowances for hems, headings and, where applicable, styling allowances, such as for the pouf on a balloon shade. These allowances are listed on the item page under the corresponding yardage calculation. Next, multiply this amount by the number of widths required and divide by 36 to obtain the number of yards. This calculation applies only to solid fabrics or to fabrics that a have a pattern repeat of less than six inches.

OR (to calculate the yardage for a fabric with a pattern repeat of more than six inches)

Step 2b) Add the length and applicable allowances together and divide by the pattern repeat. This figure is the number of pattern repeats that are required to achieve the desired length. If this number is a fraction it must be rounded upward to the nearest whole number.

Step 2c) Determine the cut length- this is the actual length that the workroom will cut the fabric after allowing for pattern repeats, hems, etc. Multiply the number of repeats required by the size of the pattern repeat. This number is the cut length.

Step 2d) Multiply the number of widths required, as calculated in Step 1, by the cut length. Divide by 36 to obtain the total yardage required for a pattern repeat.

Note: Every attempt has been made to ensure the accuracy of the calculations and yardage charts of the items in this book. However, variations in fabrics or workroom specifications may require certain modifications to the yardage calculations. Please consult your workroom.

If the glass is:	Total stack back should be:	Rod length & drapery coverage should be:
38"	26"	64"
48"	28"	72"
50"	30"	80"
56"	32"	88"
62"	34"	96"
68"	36"	104"
75"	37"	112"
81"	38"	120"
87"	41"	128"
94"	42"	136"
100"	44"	144"
108"	46"	152"
112"	48"	160"
119"	49"	168"
125"	51"	176"
131"	53"	184"
137"	55"	192"
144"	56"	200"
150"	58"	208"
158"	60"	216"
162"	62"	224"
169"	63"	232"
176"	66"	240"
181"	67"	248"
187"	69"	255"

Note: *You will have to add returns and overlaps to drapery coverage. This chart is based on average pleating and medium-weight fabric. You may deduct 7" from rod length if you are using a one-way rod. If bulky fabric is used, add 10%.*

Pleat to/Fullness Chart

(48" fabric) 2½ times fullness														
Pleat to	19	38	57	76	95	114	133	152	171	190	209	228	247	266	285
Widths	1	2	3	4	5	6	7	8	9	10	11	12	13	14	15

(48" fabric) 3 times fullness														
Pleat to	15	30	45	60	75	90	105	120	135	150	165	180	195	210	225
Widths	1	2	3	4	5	6	7	8	9	10	11	12	13	14	15

(54" fabric) 2½ times fullness														
Pleat to	21	42	63	84	105	126	147	168	189	210	231	254	273	294	315
Widths	1	2	3	4	5	6	7	8	9	10	11	12	13	14	15

(54" fabric) 3 times fullness														
Pleat to	17	34	51	68	85	102	119	136	153	170	187	204	221	238	255
Widths	1	2	3	4	5	6	7	8	9	10	11	12	13	14	15

YARDAGE CHART

Yardage Chart for 4" or 5" heading (Cut plus 20")
Total number of widths per pair or panel

Finished length

	2W	3W	4W	5W	6W	7W	8W	9W	10W	11W	12W	13W	14W	15W
36"	3¼	4¾	6¼	7¾	9¼	10¾	12¼	13¾	15¼	16¾	18¼	19¾	21¼	22¾
40"	3½	5	6½	8	9½	11	12½	14	15½	17	18½	20	21½	23
44"	3¾	5½	7¼	9	10¾	12½	14¼	16	17¾	19½	21¼	23	24¾	26½
48"	4	5¾	7½	9¼	11	12¾	14½	16¼	18	19¾	21½	23¼	25	26¾
52"	4	6	8	10	12	14	16	18	20	22	24	26	28	30
56"	4¼	6½	8½	10¾	12¾	15	16¾	19	21¼	23¼	25½	27½	29¾	31¾
60"	4½	6¾	9	11¼	13½	15¾	18	20	22¼	24½	26¾	29	31¼	33½
64"	4¾	7	9½	11¾	14	16½	18¾	21	23½	25¾	28	30½	32¾	35
68"	5	7½	10	12¼	14¾	17¼	19¾	22	24½	27	29½	32	34¼	36¾
72"	5¼	7¾	10¼	13	15½	18	20.5	23	25¾	28¼	30¾	33¼	36	38½
76"	5½	8	10¾	13½	16	18¾	21.5	24	26¾	29½	32	34¾	37½	40
80"	5¾	8½	11¼	14	16¾	19½	22¼	25	28	30¾	33½	36¼	39	41¾
84"	6	8¾	11¾	14½	17.5	20¼	23¼	26	29	32	34¾	37¾	40½	43½
88"	6	9	12	15	18	21	24	27	30	33	36	39	42	45
92"	6¼	9½	12½	15¾	18¾	22	25	28	31¼	34¼	37½	40½	43¾	46¾
96"	6½	9¾	13	16¼	19½	22¾	26	29	32¼	35½	38¾	42	45¼	48½
100"	6¾	10	13½	16¾	20	23½	26¾	30	33½	36¾	40	43½	46¾	50
104"	7	10½	14	17¼	20¾	24¼	27¾	31	34½	38	41½	45	48¼	51¾
108"	7¼	10¾	14¼	18	21½	25	28.5	32	35¾	39¼	42¾	46¼	50	53½

RTB...Cut plus 12"   Tiebacks...Cut plus 12"
Yardage chart for 5" headings (double) . . .plain fabrics only. Cut plus 20"

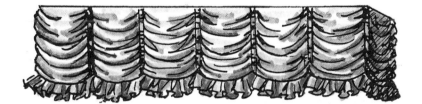

WHETHER ALONE OR AS AN ACCOMPANIMENT to an existing window treatment, valances, cornices, swags and other top treatments are an exquisite addition to any home. Some top treatments, such as the casual scarf valance, will step into a supporting role alongside an elegant set of draperies or a modest vertical blind. Other top treatments: the majestic swags, the sumptuous lambrequins, will command a room, drawing the spotlight upon themselves so that all may enjoy their stand-alone beauty. From the most petite bathroom window to a large picture window, top treatments are the answer to any window dressing question.

Swags and cascades with Maltese Cross

Swags and cascades over pleated draperies
and Roman shade

Swag and cascade over pleated valance

Various swag embellishments

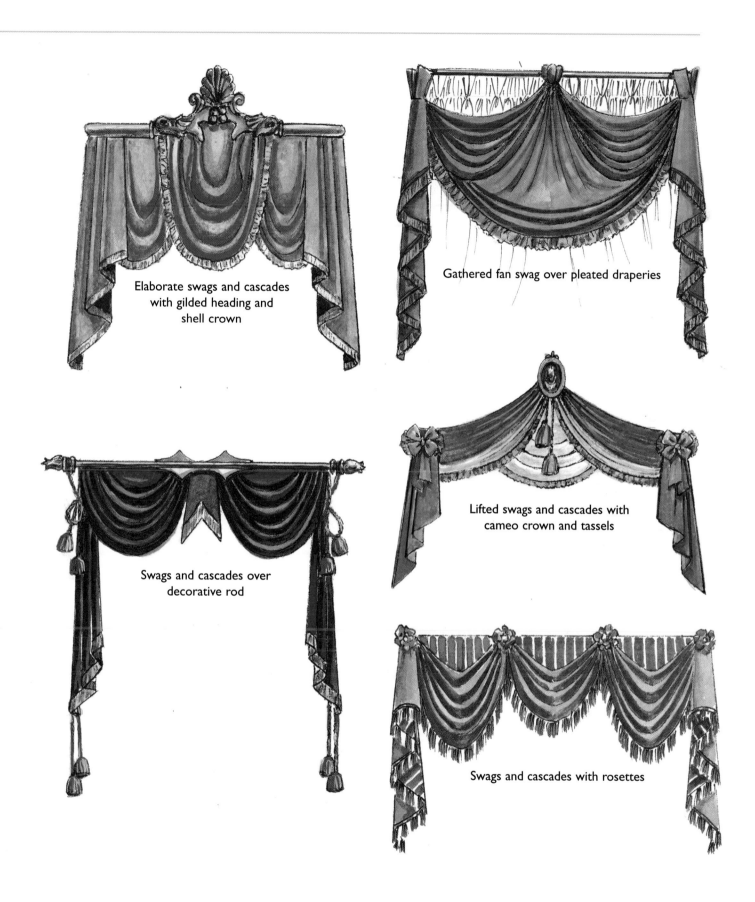

Elaborate swags and cascades
with gilded heading and
shell crown

Gathered fan swag over pleated draperies

Swags and cascades over
decorative rod

Lifted swags and cascades with
cameo crown and tassels

Swags and cascades with rosettes

Swags and cascades over rod pocket valance

Swags and cascades over designer cornice

Various swag and cascade combinations

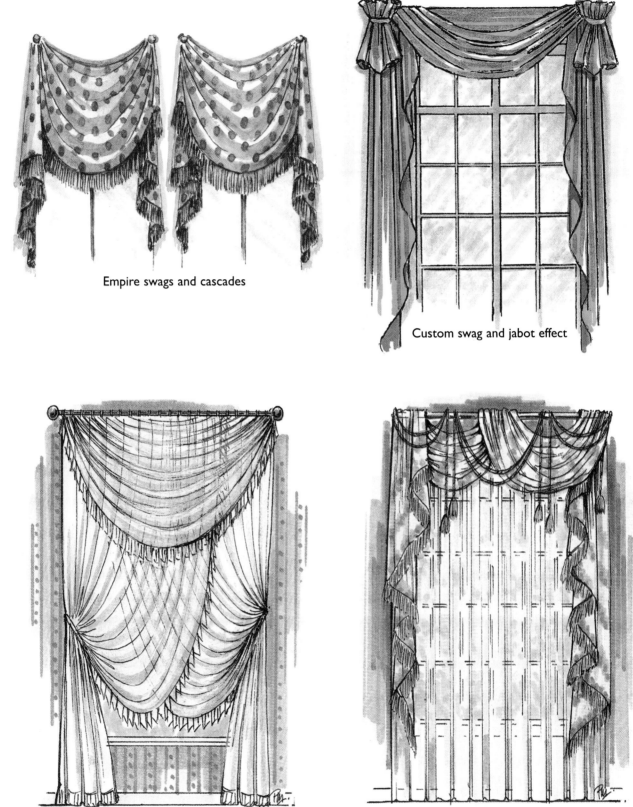

Empire swags and cascades

Custom swag and jabot effect

Deep swag and full tiebacks

Fabric swagged over a pole with cord and tassel trim

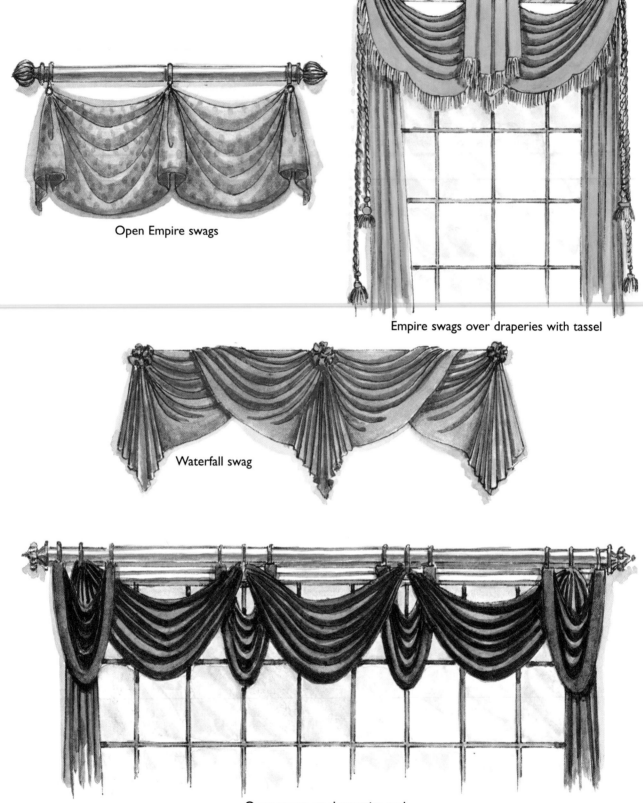

Open Empire swags

Empire swags over draperies with tassel

Waterfall swag

Open swags on decorative rod

Raised swags over
tiebacks

Sheer swag with knots

Swags over decorative rod with inverted cascades

Swag and jabot with tassels
and rope

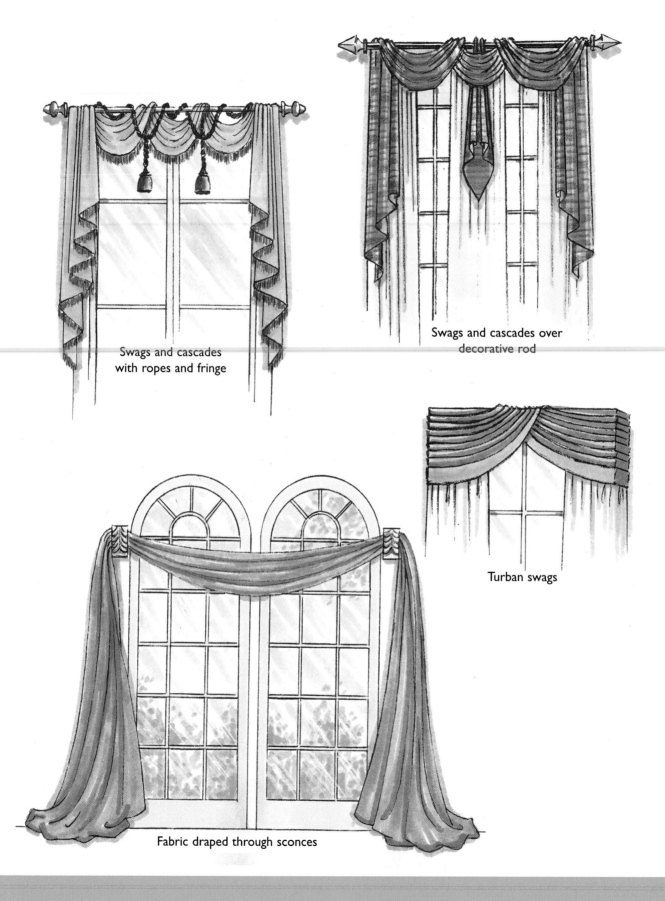

Swags and cascades
with ropes and fringe

Swags and cascades over
decorative rod

Turban swags

Fabric draped through sconces

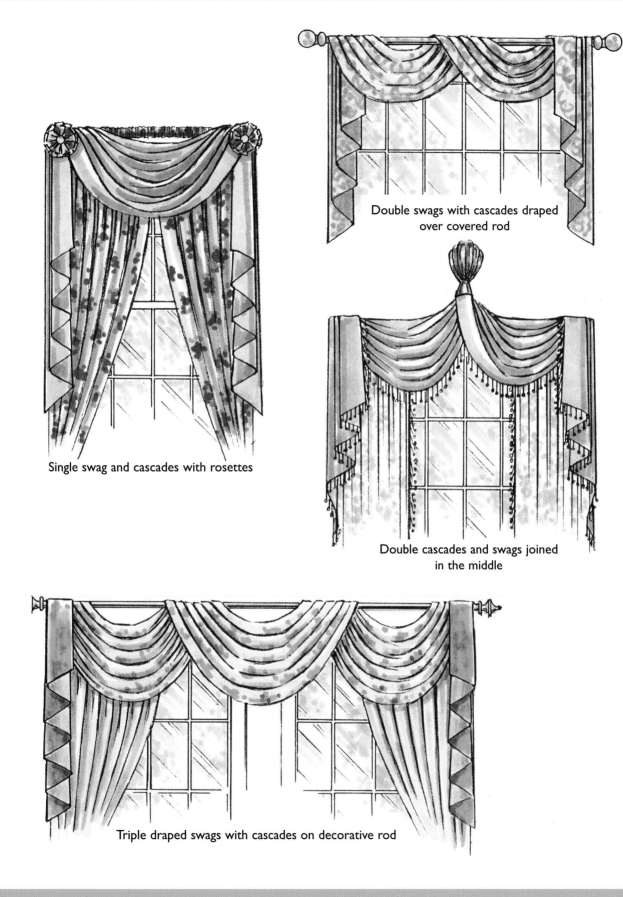

Double swags with cascades draped
over covered rod

Single swag and cascades with rosettes

Double cascades and swags joined
in the middle

Triple draped swags with cascades on decorative rod

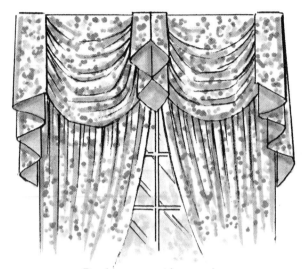

Double swag with cascades

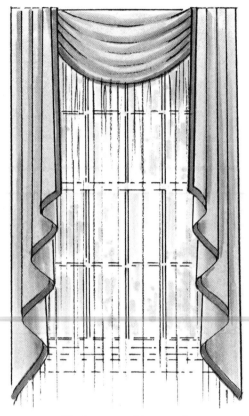

Single swag with cascades

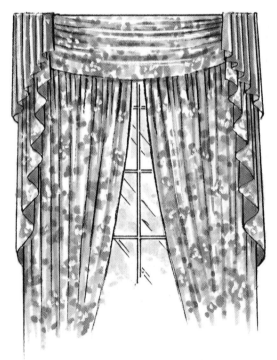

Long single swag with two tiers of cascades

Angled double swags and cascades with rosettes

Double swags crossed in middle with four
single cascades on rings

Double swags with ruffles
and bows over cascades

Asymmetric swags and cascades

Swags and cascades with knots and tassels

Liner swags and cascades

Swags and rosettes and center jabot

Swag with Maltese Cross ties

Gathered swag

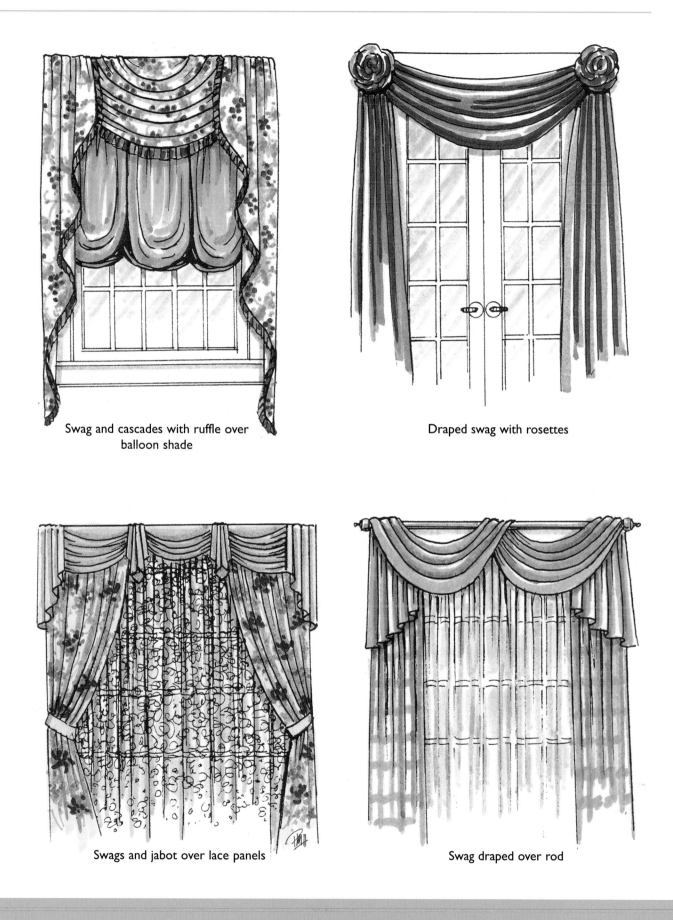

Swag and cascades with ruffle over
balloon shade

Draped swag with rosettes

Swags and jabot over lace panels

Swag draped over rod

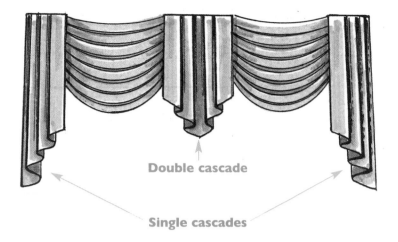

Double cascade

Single cascades

Empire Swag with Jabots

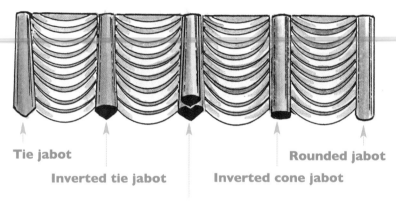

Tie jabot

Inverted tie jabot

Rounded jabot

Inverted cone jabot

Double inverted tie jabot

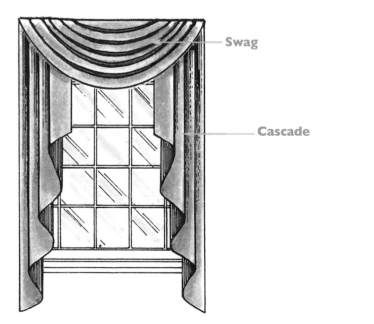

Swag

Cascade

Swag and cascades with ties

Swag with rosettes and cascades

Double swag with rosettes and cascades

Ruffled swag over tiebacks

Double swag with cascades and pleated edge

Ruffled balloon swag

Swag with asymmetric cascades

Boxed swag valance

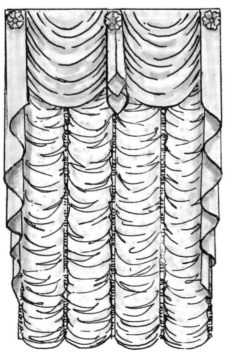

Swags over Austrian shade

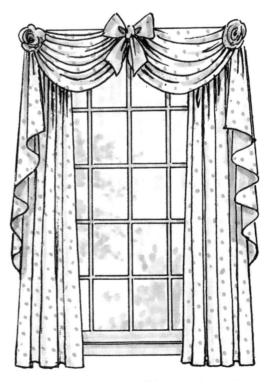

Swag with rosettes and bow in the middle

Draped swag with contrasting lining

Swag with lifted center and cascading tails

Double swagged valance

Single swag with rosettes

Swag and cascade arrangement styles

Swag and cascade arrangement styles

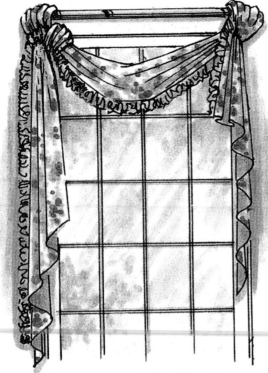

Asymmetric swag held by fabric ties

Fabric swagged through large brass rings

Swagged fabric with cord trim over
asymmetric tieback

Draperies over bay window with large swags held by bows

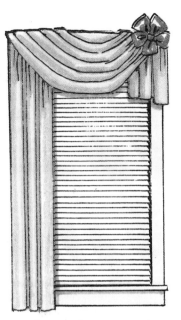

Swag with rosette and
asymmetric cascades

Double swag with plain cascades over print

Swags and long cascades over French doors

Box pleated valance with buttons

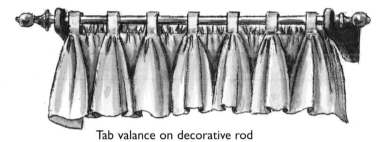

Tab valance on decorative rod

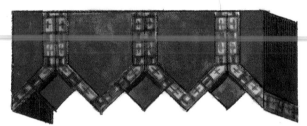

Box pleated valance with points and banding

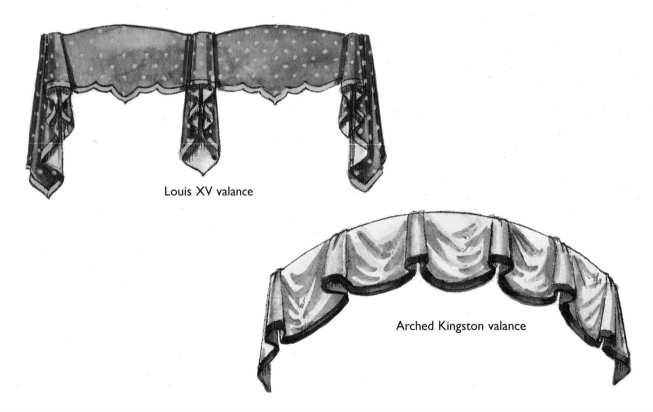

Louis XV valance

Arched Kingston valance

Murphy valance

Bordeaux valance

Arched box pleated valance
with heading

Multi-point valance with pleats and fringe

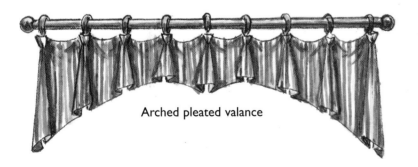

Arched pleated valance

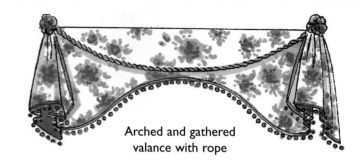

Arched and gathered
valance with rope

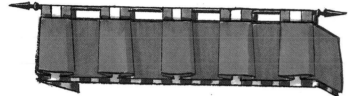

Box pleated valance with tabs

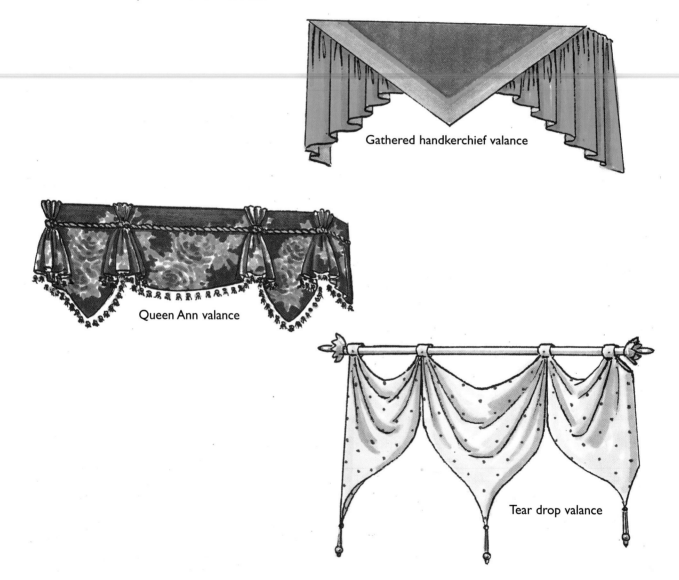

Gathered handkerchief valance

Queen Ann valance

Tear drop valance

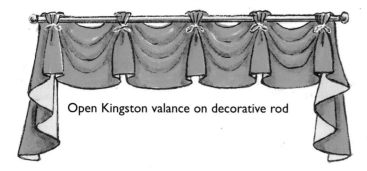

Open Kingston valance on decorative rod

Multi-level box pleated valance

Soft cornice with banners

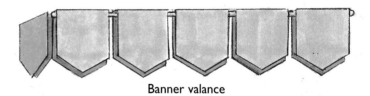

Banner valance

Scalloped tabbed valance with trim

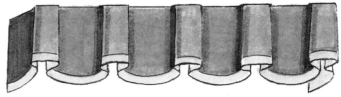

Regal valance

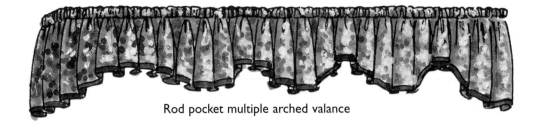

Rod pocket multiple arched valance

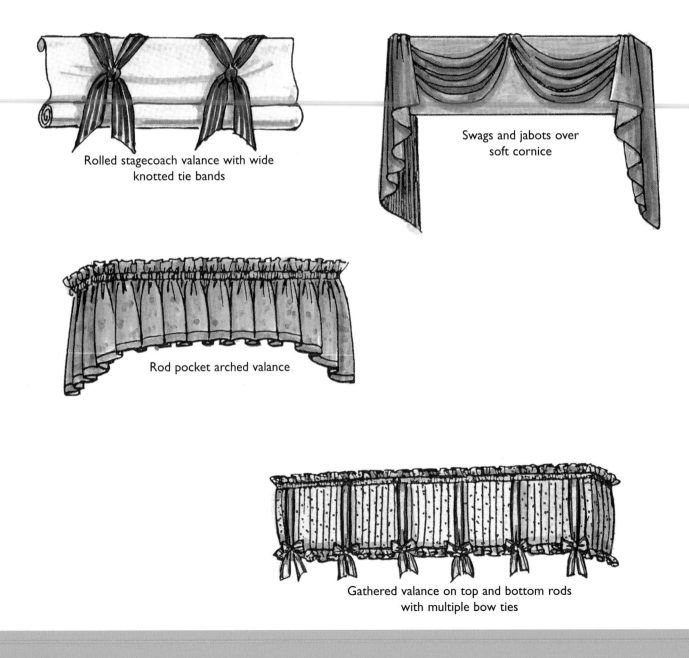

Rolled stagecoach valance with wide
knotted tie bands

Swags and jabots over
soft cornice

Rod pocket arched valance

Gathered valance on top and bottom rods
with multiple bow ties

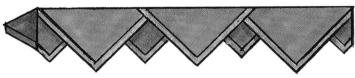

Multiple point valance with edge banding

Box pleated valance with twisted cording

Triple cone pleated valance on decorative rod

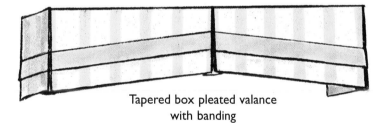

Tapered box pleated valance
with banding

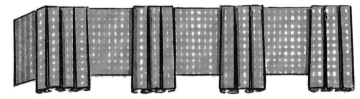

Valance with triple box pleats

Swags and cascades over lambrequin valance

Balloon shade with double knotted cords

Shaped valance with triple knots

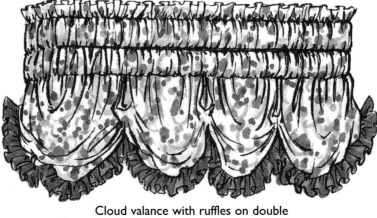

Cloud valance with ruffles on double
flat rods

Gathered valance under narrow cornice with bows at corners

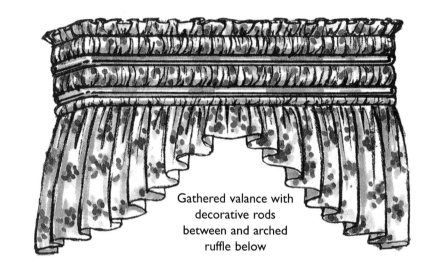

Gathered valance with
decorative rods
between and arched
ruffle below

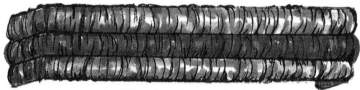

Triple 4½" gathered flat rod valance

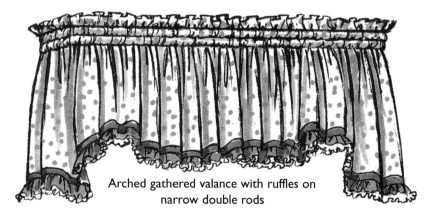

Arched gathered valance with ruffles on
narrow double rods

Two gathered valances on flat rods with
decorative rod in middle

Gathered valance on flat rod with decorative rods
at top and botom

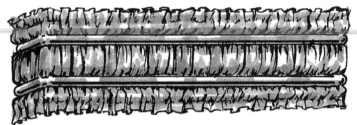

Gathered valance with flat rod in middle and two
decorative rods between

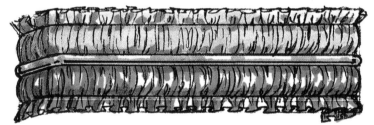

Two 4½" flat rods with decorative rod in middle

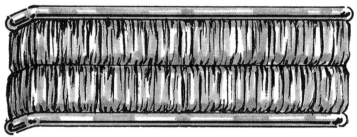

Two 4½" flat rods with decorative rods top and bottom

Double pinch pleat

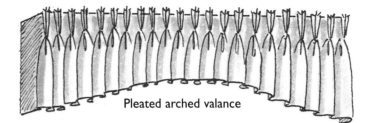

Pleated arched valance

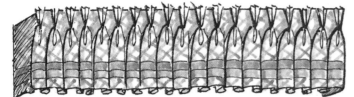

French pleated valance

Double pleat Queen Ann

Space pleated valance

Queen Ann valance

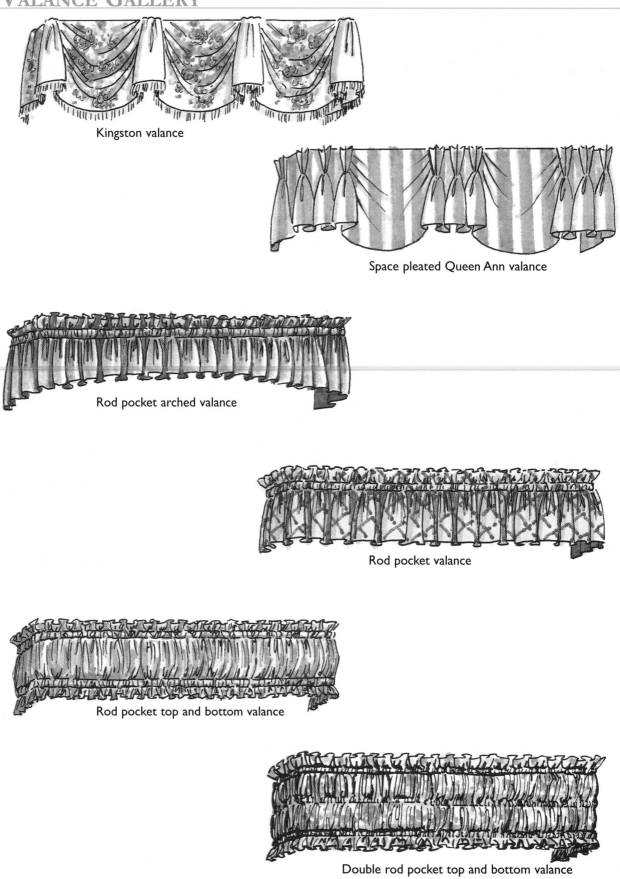

Kingston valance

Space pleated Queen Ann valance

Rod pocket arched valance

Rod pocket valance

Rod pocket top and bottom valance

Double rod pocket top and bottom valance

Double rod pocket top and bottom valance

Rod pocket top and bottom valance with lower
rod lifted

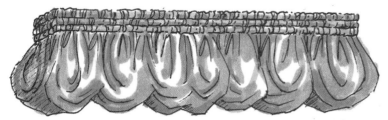

Cloud valance with shirred heading

Cloud valance with rod pocket heading

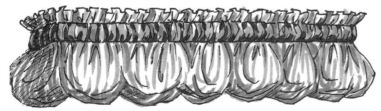

Cloud valance with stand-up ruffle

Balloon valance with piping

Rod top swag and cascade

Rod pocket tapered valance

Rod pocket swag and jabot valance

Austrian valance with fringe

Austrian valance with jabots

Austrian valance with cascades

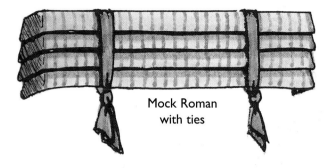

Mock Roman
with ties

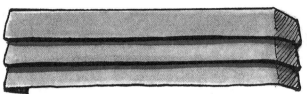

Mock Roman

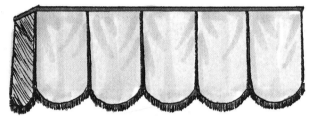

Scalloped valance with fringed edge

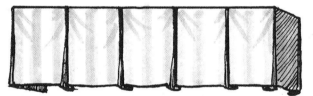

Inverted box pleat

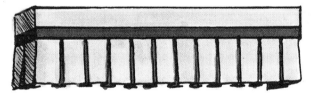

Inverted box pleat with banding

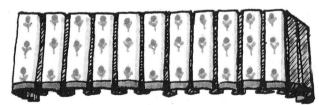

Box pleat with banding

Rod pocket with stand-up ruffle

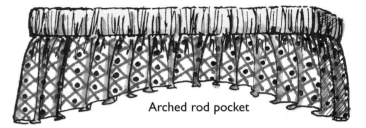

Arched rod pocket

Double rod pocket with stand-up top
and bottom

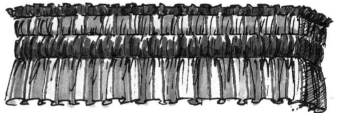

Double rod pocket with stand-up top

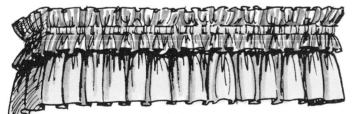

Double ruffled valance shirred on rod

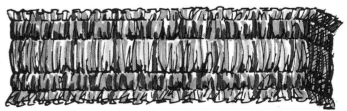

Double rod pocket top and bottom with stand-up
top and bottom

Rod pocket heading with no stand-up

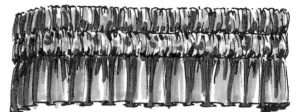

Double rod pocket with no stand-up

Double rod pocket cloud valance

Triple rod pocket with multiple fabrics

Four-inch shirred heading

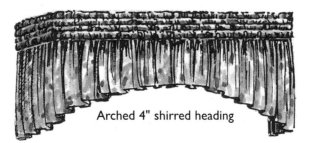

Arched 4" shirred heading

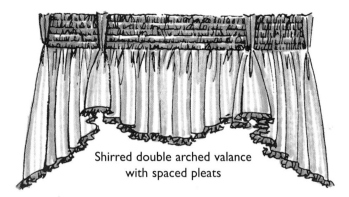

Shirred double arched valance
with spaced pleats

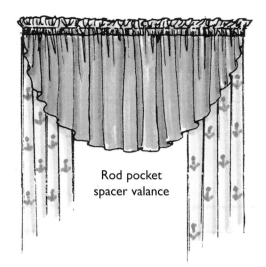

Rod pocket
spacer valance

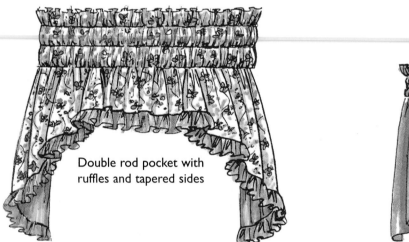

Double rod pocket with
ruffles and tapered sides

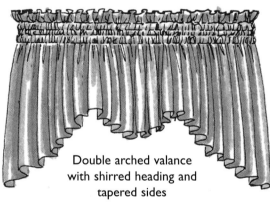

Double arched valance
with shirred heading and
tapered sides

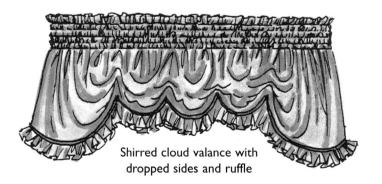

Shirred cloud valance with
dropped sides and ruffle

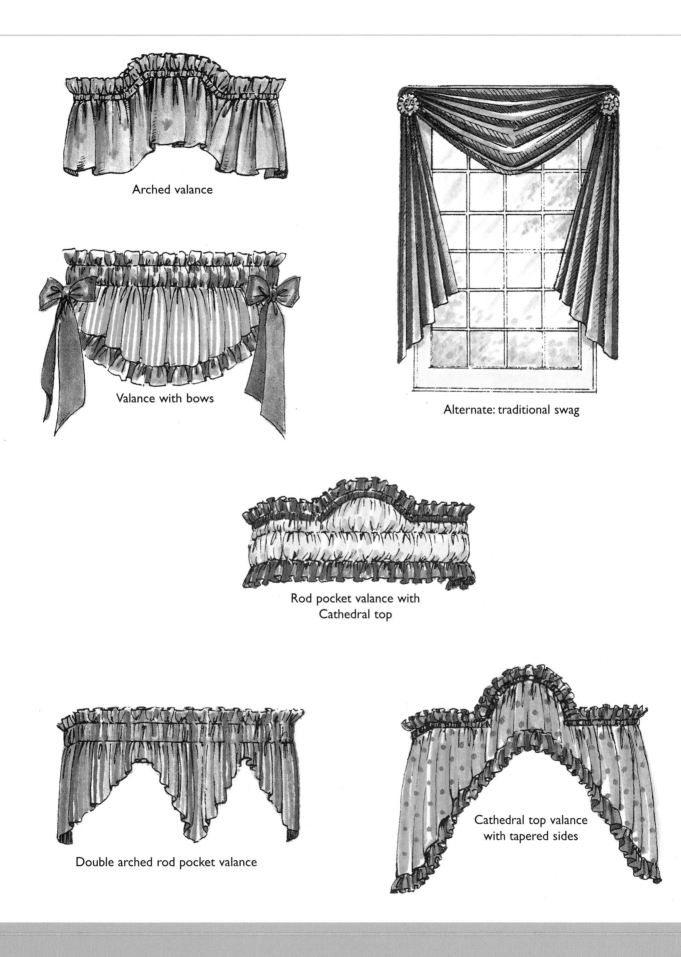

Arched valance

Valance with bows

Alternate: traditional swag

Rod pocket valance with
Cathedral top

Double arched rod pocket valance

Cathedral top valance
with tapered sides

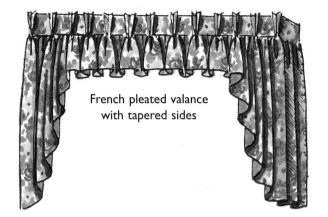

French pleated valance
with tapered sides

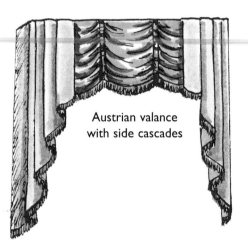

Austrian valance
with side cascades

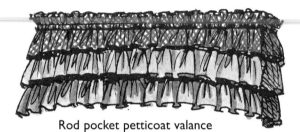

Rod pocket petticoat valance

New Orleans
valance with 6"
ruffle

Rod pocket
valance with
tapered sides

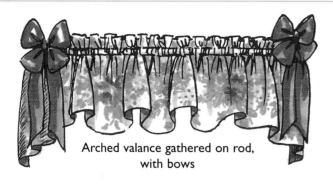

Arched valance gathered on rod,
with bows

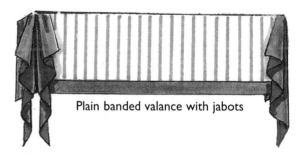

Cloud valance with stand-up ruffle

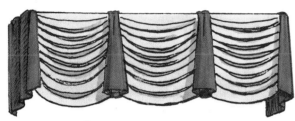

Empire valance with jabots

Plain banded valance with jabots

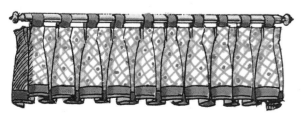

Tab top valance on decorative rod

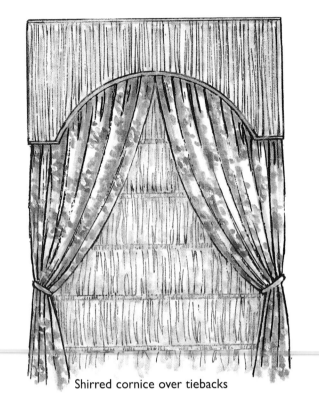

Shirred cornice over tiebacks

Lambrequin with welt edge over Roman shade

Shirred lambrequin over pleated drapery

Cornice box with shirred band
and ruffled cascade

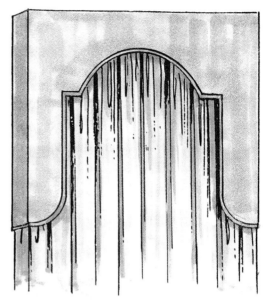

Shaped cornice box with vertical side drops

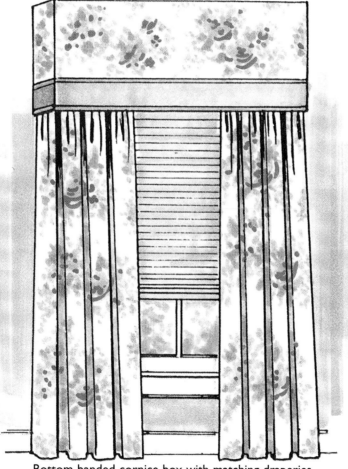

Bottom banded cornice box with matching draperies

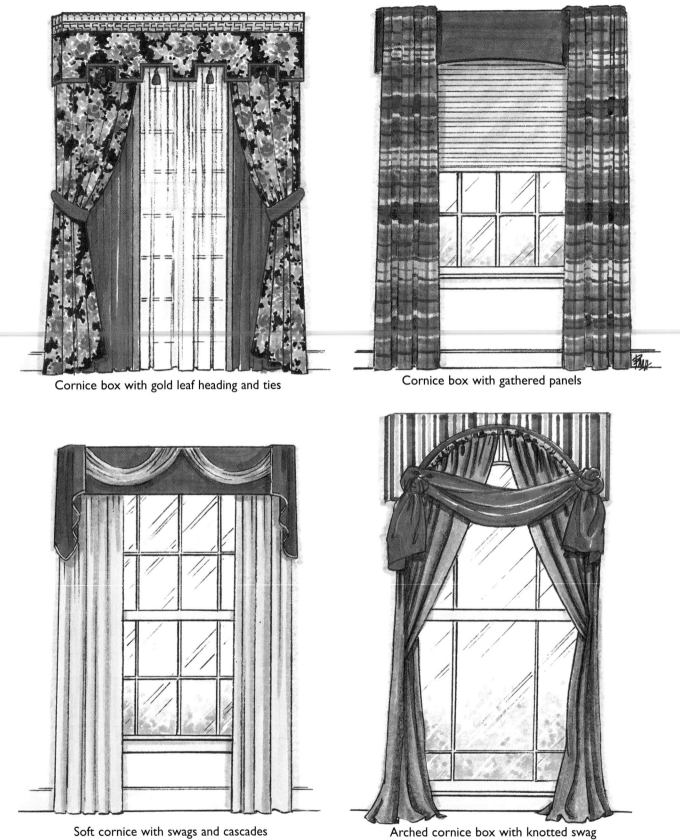

Cornice box with gold leaf heading and ties

Cornice box with gathered panels

Soft cornice with swags and cascades

Arched cornice box with knotted swag

Various lambrequin shapes

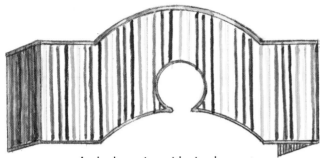

Arched cornice with circular center

Cornice with banding top and appliqué

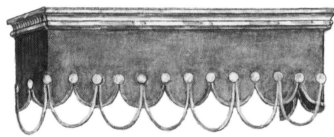

Cornice box with gilded top and rope tassels

Designer gilded wood top cornice

Cornice box with large rope top and appliqué

Cornice box with appliqué

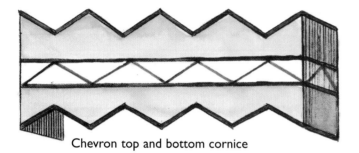

Chevron top and bottom cornice

Pagoda cornice

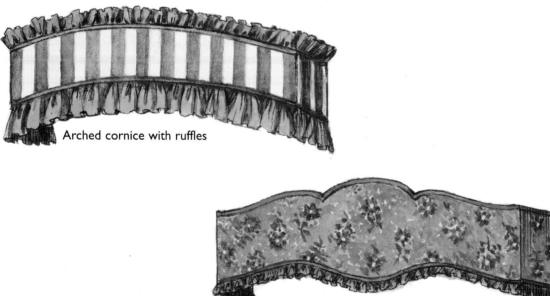

Arched cornice with ruffles

Custom design cornice with bottom ruffle

Button swagged cornice

Shaped crown cornice with gathered valance

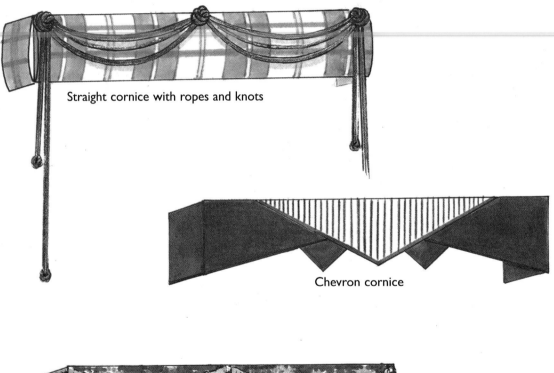

Straight cornice with ropes and knots

Chevron cornice

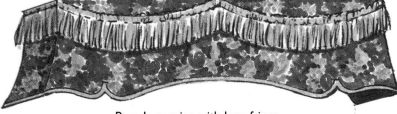

Pagoda cornice with long fringe

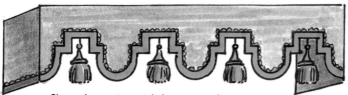

Shaped cornice with large tassels

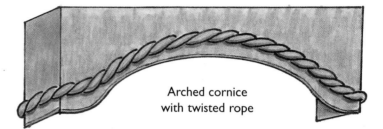

Arched cornice
with twisted rope

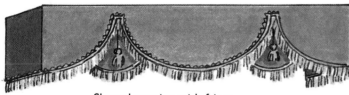

Shaped cornice with fringe

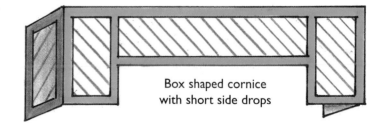

Box shaped cornice
with short side drops

Multi-fabric cornice

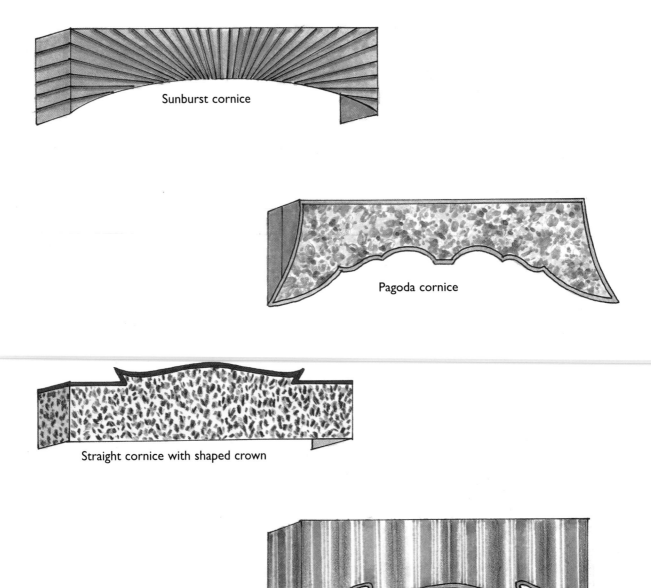

Sunburst cornice

Pagoda cornice

Straight cornice with shaped crown

Custom shaped cornice

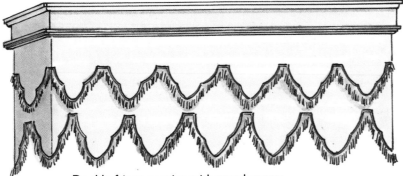

Double fringe cornice with wood crown

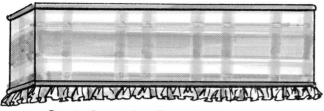

Cornice box with ruffle on bottom

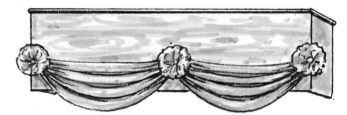

Cornice box with swag and rosettes

Cornice box with shirred and flat panels

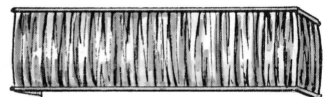

Shirred cornice box

Cornice box with gathered fabric in middle

Wood cornice with painted leaf design

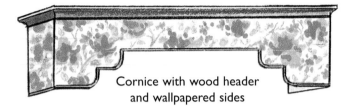

Cornice with wood header
and wallpapered sides

Straight cornice with stenciled design

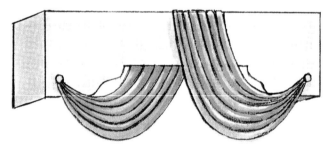

Cornice with in-and-out swag

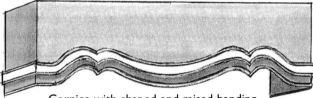

Cornice with shaped and raised banding

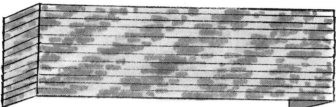

Cornice with honeycomb pleating

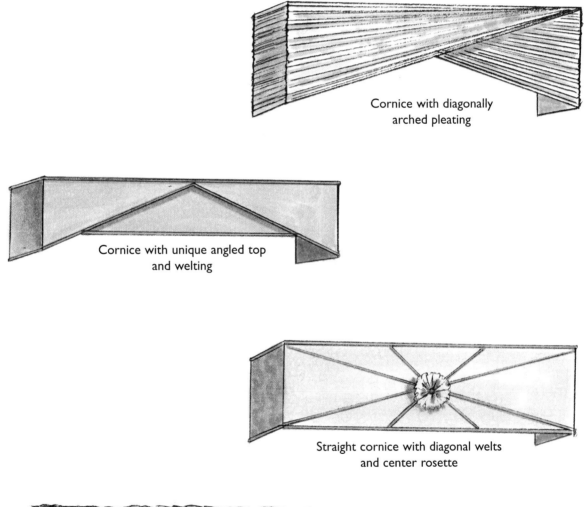

Cornice with diagonally
arched pleating

Cornice with unique angled top
and welting

Straight cornice with diagonal welts
and center rosette

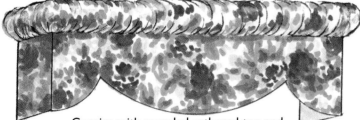

Cornice with rounded gathered top and
large scalloped bottom

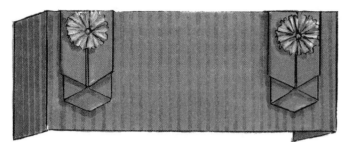

Straight cornice with rosettes and jabots

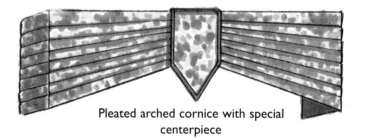

Pleated arched cornice with special centerpiece

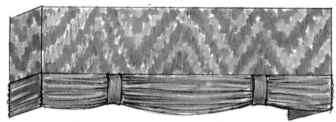

Cornice with unique pleated bottom

Straight cornice with gathered hourglass and rosette accent

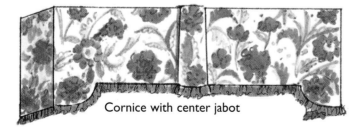

Cornice with center jabot

Cornice box with shirred bottom band

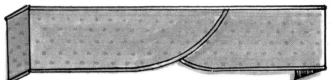

Cornice box with special welting

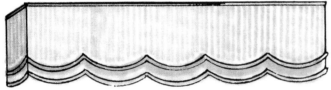

Scalloped bottom with banding

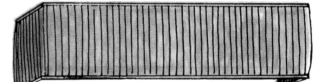

Cornice box with one-inch pleats

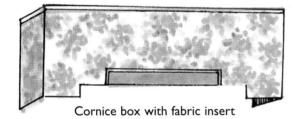

Cornice box with fabric insert

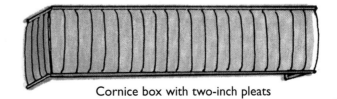

Cornice box with two-inch pleats

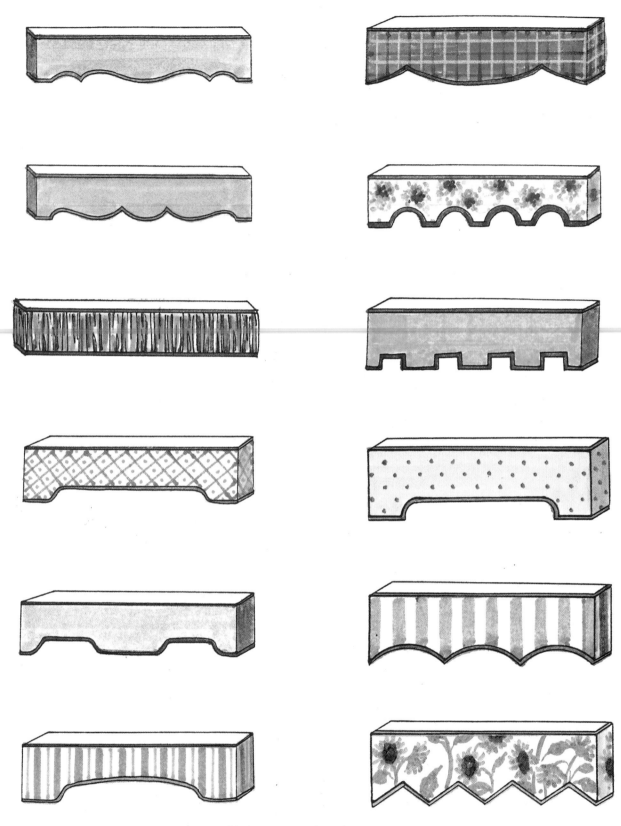

Various cornice box shapes

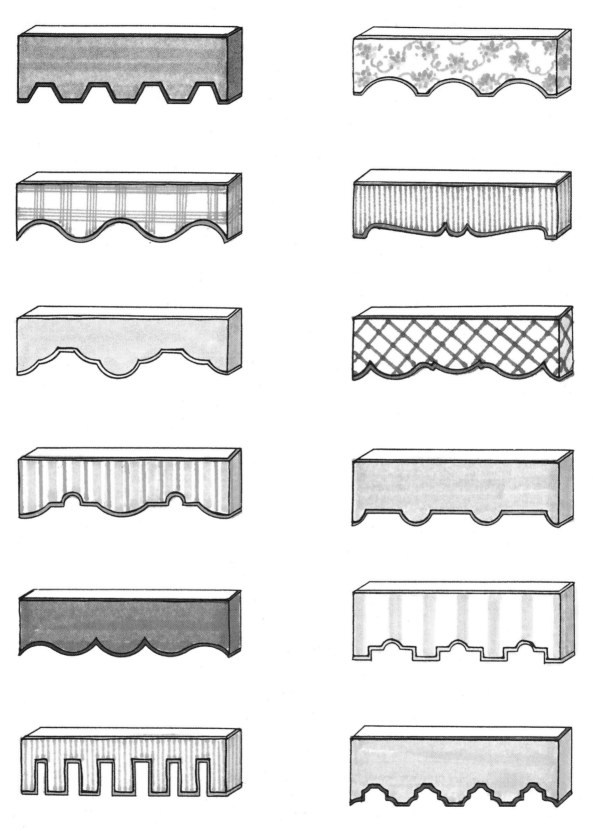

Various cornice box shapes

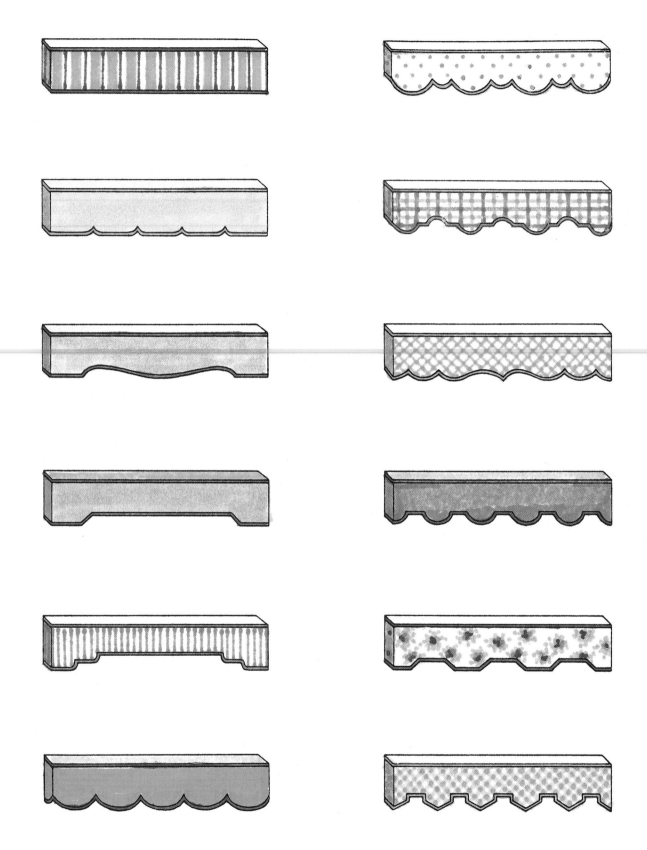

Various cornice box shapes

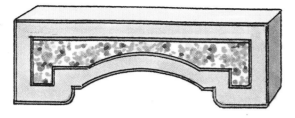

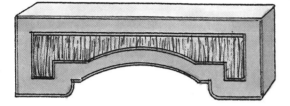

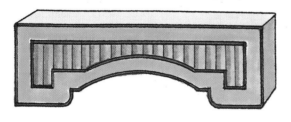

General Information:

Cornices and lambrequins are padded with polyester fiberfill and constructed of wood or chipboard.

Non-directional and solid fabrics should be railroaded to eliminate seams. matching welting is standard on all cornices ad is applied to the top and bottom edges. Coordinating colors for welting has a more dramatic effect.

When ordering to fit tight applications, (i.e. wall to wall, bay windows, for example), be sure to measure at the elevation of this installation. "Exact outside face measurement—wall to wall installation." Allow one inch for clearance.

Measuring:

Measure drapery rod from end bracket to end bracket and add four inches for rod clearance and cornice/lambrequin. Six inch returns are needed when mounted over a single rod and eight-inch returns when mounted over a double rod.

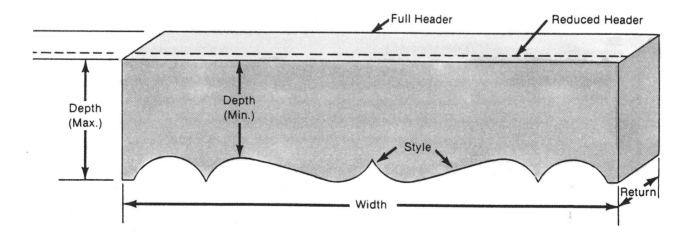

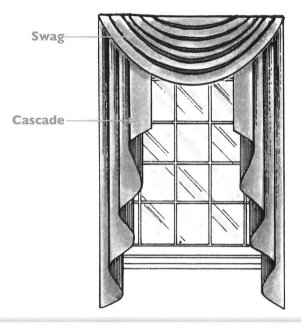

Swag

Cascade

Description—Swags: Swags are top treatments or balances, used over draperies or blinds, or sometimes alone. They are usually draped into soft, graceful folds, using fabrics that drape easily. It is more interesting to use an odd number of swags. Swags should be lined.

Yardage:

Based on an average of 44" per swag, you will need two yards of fabric per swag.

Swag Width, Board Face & Number of Swags:

Swags may vary in width from 20" to over 70". Very small swags have only a few folds. Extremely wide swags will have a limited drop length. The width of the swag is determined by the board face and the number of swags that will be used on each treatment. The following guide (*right*) will help determine thenumber of swags needed, based on the board face. The guide is based on the assumption that swag overlap will start approximately one-half or less the width of the swag face.

Swag Width:

To find the width of each swag, divide the board face by one or more than the number of swags used and multiply by 2.
Example:
Boards face width = 127".
Number of swags = 5
127" ÷ 5 = 25.4 x 2 = 50.8 or 51" width for each swag.

Standard Drop Length:

The standard drop lengths of swags are 16", 18" or 20". usually six or seven folds are placed across the top of a traditional swag with a standard drop. Swags that have shallow drops of 12" will have three or four folds.

The chart (*right*) is an average guide to help you in finding swag drop based on face width.

If board face is:	# of swags to determine are:
36" to 48"	1 swag
49" to 70"	2 swags
71" to 100"	3 swags
101" to 125"	4 swags
126" to 150"	5 swags
151" to 175"	6 swags
176" to 200"	7 swags
201" to 225"	8 swags
226" to 250"	9 swags
251" to 275"	10 swags
276" to 300"	11 swags

If swag face width is:	Average drop will be:
20"	10" to 13"
25"	12" to 17"
30"	14" to 19"
35"	14" to 20"
40"	14" to 21"
45"	16" to 23"
50"	16" to 23"
Over 60"	16" to 24"

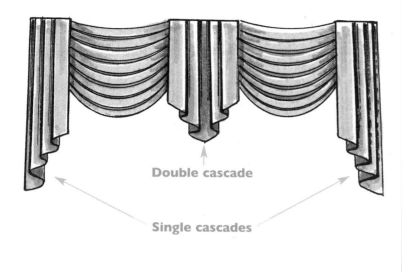

Double cascade

Single cascades

Empire Swag with Jabots

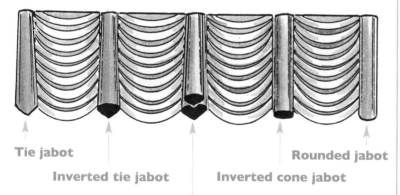

Tie jabot

Inverted tie jabot

Double inverted tie jabot

Inverted cone jabot

Rounded jabot

Description—Cascades:

Cascades are folded pieces of fabric that fall from the top of the drapery heading or valance to create a zig-zag effect. Cascades muct be lined with the cover fabric or one that contrasts.

Yardage:

Double the longest length + 4" ÷ 36. This will give you the number of yards needed for a single pair of cascades.

Single Traditional Cascade:

(Yardage is for one cascade only)

<u>Lined in contrasting fabric:</u>

<u>Length:</u>

Cut length of face = finished length (long point) + 4" extra

<u>Width:</u>

Allow one width for face and one width for lining

<u>Self-lined:</u>

<u>Length:</u>

Finished length (long point) x 2 + 4" = cut length of face and lining

<u>Width:</u>

One width will accomodate face and lining

Double Cascade:

<u>Length:</u>

Contrast or self-lined: Finished length + 4" = cut length

<u>Width:</u>

(Face) One width per double cascade (up to 14")

(Lining) One width per double cascade

Description—Jabots:

Jabots are decorative pieces of fabric that are ung over seams or between swags on a valance. Jabots may be tie shaped, cone shaped or rounded on the bottom.

Yardage:

Allow approximately one third yard of fabric for each jabot.

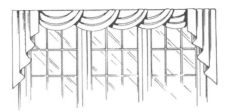

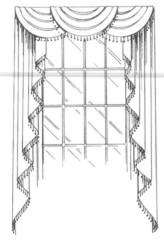

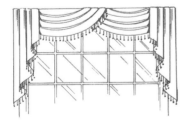

Specifications

Description:

Overlapping swags draped gracefully across the width of the window make an elegant and formal window treatment. Jabots, the decorative side pieces, are constructed to create a cascading effect.

Yardage:

Swags:
 1½ yards each

Jabots:
 Finished length of jabot ÷ 10" x 2 ÷ 36 = yardage with pattern repeat
 —or—
 Finished length of jabot + 10" + pattern repeat; allow same yardage for contrast or self-lining in jabots.

Work Order Specifications:

1. Swag formation: Traditional, Regency or Georgian style
2. Color of lining in swags
3. Contrast or self-lining jabots
4. Width, length of swags, length of jabots
5. Number of swags
6. Returns

Special Note:

1. Each swag is constructed approximately 30" wide. When overlapped, the area a swag covers is approximately 20".
2. A check measure and installation are strongly recommended.
3. Not recommended for bay windows. See linear swags.

Specifications

Description:

Swags are draped beautifully across the window and can be used with a decorative rod and constructed to appear as if the fabric is thrown casually over the rod or constructed as one large swag that is mounted on wood.

Yardage:

<u>One swag</u>

Width of the window + 30% ÷ 36 = yardage

<u>More than one swag</u>

Width of the window + 50% ÷ 36 = yardage

<u>Jabots</u>

Length of jabots + 10" x 2 ÷ 36 = yardage without pattern repeat

—or—

Length of jabots + 10" + pattern repeat x 2 ÷ 36 = yardage with pattern repeat; allow some yardage for contrast or self-lining in jabots and swags

Work Order Specifications:

1. Color of lining in swags
2. Lining of jabots: self-lined or contrast
3. Width, length of swags and jabots
4. Number of swags
5. Wood and hook and loop fastener mount or decorative rod

Special Note:

1. These swags are cut on a straight grain of fabric. Any fabric with an obvious directional print is not suitable.
2. Proportions are very important with this type of swag.
3. Check measure and installation are strongly recommended.
4. Not applicable for bay windows.

Specifications

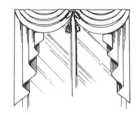

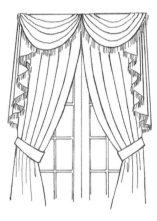

Description:

Most commonly used in a bay window where overlapping swags are inappropriate. Swags are butted together and sewn end to end. Decorative cascades and/or rosettes are used to conceal the seams of the swags and the heading of underdrapes. Jabots are used as the finishing touches on each end.

Yardage:

<u>Swags:</u>

18" to 30" wide: 1½ yards each

<u>Cascades:</u>

1½ yards each

<u>Jabots:</u>

Length of jabot + 10" x 2 ÷ 36 = yardage without pattern repeat

—or—

Length of jabot + 10" + pattern repeat x 2 ÷ 36 = yardage with pattern repeat; allow same yardage of contrast or self-lining in jabots.

Work Order Specifications:

1. Color of lining in swags
2. Contrast or self-lining jabots
3. Width, length of swags, jabots and cascades
4. Number of swags
5. Returns

Special Note:

To achieve proper proportions, consult with workroom.

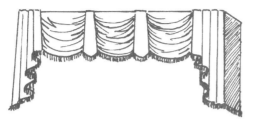

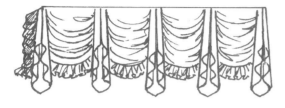

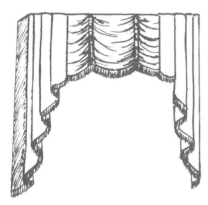

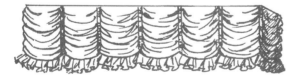

Specifications

Description:
A soft, formal valance created by vertical shirring between scallops. Combine with other treatments to create a complete look.

Yardage:

Step 1
Width of area to be covered + returns x 1.5 ÷ width of fabric = number of widths (whole numbers only)

Step 2a
Number of widths x (length of valance x 3) ÷ 36 = yardage without pattern repeat
—or—

Step 2b
Length of valance x 3 ÷ pattern repeat = number of repeats required (round upward to nearest whole number)

Step 2c
Number of repeats required x pattern repeat = cut length

Step 2d
Number of widths x cut length ÷ 36 = yardage with pattern repeat

Work Order Specifications:
1. Width
2. Length
3. Color of lining
4. Inside or outside mount
5. Returns

Special Note:
1. This is a stationary treatment.
2. This treatment cannot be used when treatment underneath is mounted up to the ceiling.
3. Extra yardage has to be calculated for rod covers.

CLOUD VALANCE

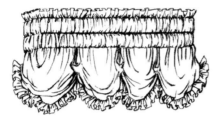

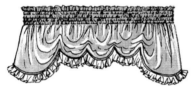

Description:
This window treatment is used to suggest a cloud shade yet it cannot be raised or lowered. Used for its softening effect on the window, the gathered heading falls into small poufs that can be finished with or without a skirt. A cloud valance can be used alone, if privacy is not a factor, or as a decorative finish over other window treatments such as vertical blinds, drapes or Venetian blinds.

Yardage:
Step 1
Width of area to be covered x 2.5 ÷ width of fabric = number of widths (whole numbers only)
Step 2a
Number of widths x (length of window + 16") ÷ 36 = yardage without pattern repeat
—or—
Step 2b
Length of valance ÷ 16" ÷ pattern repeat = number of repeats required (round upward to nearest whole number)
Step 2c
Number of repeats required x pattern repeat = cut length
Step 2d
Number of widths x cut length ÷ 36 = yardage with pattern repeat

Work Order Specifications:
1. Width
2. Length
3. Color of lining
4. Inside or outside mount
5. Skirt or no skirt
6. Size of returns or size of board
7. Ceiling or wall mount

Special Note:
For valances shorter than 16", a functional balloon that can be raised to the correct height is recommended. See balloon shade.

Savannah Valance

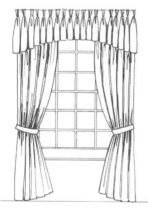

Description:

This softly shaped valance adds an interesting touch to a window without distorting the view. The Savannah valance does not dip down in the center, unlike the Legacy valance (page 169), which does. The heading may be pleated, shirred or tunneled.

Yardage:

Step 1

Width of area to be covered + returns x 2.5 ÷ width of fabric = number of widths

Step 2a

Length to longest point + 16" x number of widths ÷ 36 = yardage without pattern repeat

—or—

Step 2b

Length to longest point + 16" ÷ pattern repeat = number of repeats required (round upward to nearest whole number)

Step 2c

Number of repeats required x pattern repeat = cut length

Step 2d

Number of widths x cut length ÷ 36 = yardage with pattern repeat

Work Order Specifications:

1. Width
2. Returns
3. Length to longest point
4. Length to shortest point
5. Length to mid-point (for legacy valance)
6. Fabric details
7. Type of heading

Special Note:

A check measure and installation are strongly recommended. If using a shirred heading, a hook and loop fastener mount is recommended.

BALLOON VALANCE

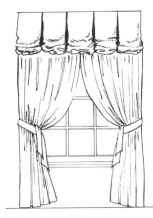

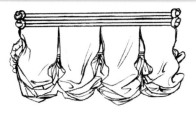

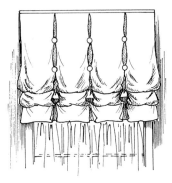

Description:
A window treatment to suggest a balloon shade yet it cannot be raised or lowered. Large inverted pleats create a more tailored effect that is softened by billowing poufs. It can be used alone, if privacy is not a factor, or as a decorative finish over other window treatments such as vertical blinds, drapes or Venetian blinds.

Yardage:
Step 1
Width of window + returns x 3 ÷ width of fabric = number of widths (whole numbers only)
Step 2a
Number of widths x (length of valance ÷ 16") ÷ 36 = yardage without pattern repeat
—or—
Step 2b
Length of valance + 16" ÷ pattern repeat = number of repeats required (round upward to nearest whole number)
Step 2c
Number of repeats required x pattern repeat = cut length
Step 2d
Number of widths x cut length ÷ 36 = yardage with pattern repeat

Work Order Specifications:
1. Width
2. Length
3. Color of lining
4. Inside or outside mount
5. Size of returns or size of board
6. Ceiling or wall mount

Special Note:
For valances shorter than 16", a functional cloud that can be raised to the correct height is recommended. *See cloud shade.*

LEGACY VALANCE

Description:
Softly shaped valances add an interesting touch to a window without distorting the view. The Legacy valance dips down in the center, unlike the Savannah valance (page 167), which does not. The heading may be pleated, shirred or tunneled.

Yardage:
Step 1
Width of area to be covered + returns x 2.5 ÷ width of fabric = number of widths
Step 2a
Length to longest point + 16" x number of widths ÷ 36 = yardage without pattern repeat
—or—
Step 2b
Length to longest point + 16" ÷ pattern repeat = number of repeats required (round upward to nearest whole number)
Step 2c
Number of repeats required x pattern repeat = cut length
Step 2d
Number of widths x cut length ÷ 36 = yardage with pattern repeat

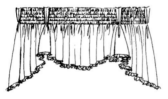

Work Order Specifications:
1. Width
2. Returns
3. Length to longest point
4. Length to shortest point
5. Length to mid-point (for legacy valance)
6. Fabric details
7. Type of heading

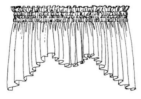

Special Note:
A check measure and installation are strongly recommended. If using a shirred heading, a hook and loop fastener mount is recommended.

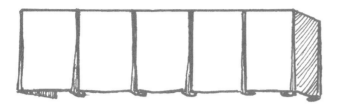

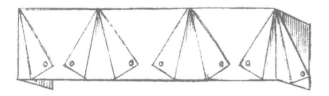

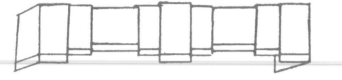

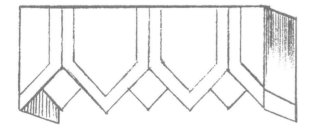

Description:

A very tailored style that lends itself well as an overtreatment with vertical blinds, Venetian blinds and tied back draperies. Contrast banding adds a crisp look.

Yardage:

Step 1

Width of area to be covered + returns x 3 ÷ width of fabric = number of widths required

Step 2a

Length of valance + 6" x number of widths ÷ 36 = yardage without pattern repeat

—or—

Step 2b

Length of valance + 6" ÷ pattern repeat = number of repeats required (round upward to nearest whole number)

Step 2c

Number of repeats required x pattern repeat = cut length

Step 2d

Number of widths x cut length ÷ 36 = yardage with pattern repeat

Work Order Specifications:

1. Width
2. Length
3. Returns
4. Color of lining
5. Contrast banding (if applicable)

Special Note:

1. A check measure and installation are strongly recommended.
2. Pleats are sized to window and pattern usually 10" to 12".

MOCK ROMAN VALANCE

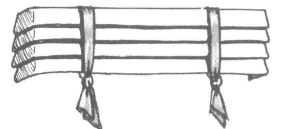

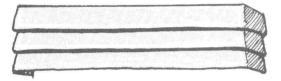

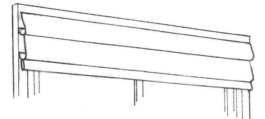

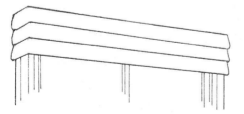

Description:

This window treatment is used to suggest a Roman shade yet it cannot be raised or lowered. A variety of decorative trims or contrast bands may be used to add interest. It is finished with two permanent pleats.

Yardage:

<u>Step 1</u>
Width of area to be covered + 4" ÷ width of fabric = number of widths required

<u>Step 2a</u>
Length + 16" x number of widths ÷ 36 = yardage without pattern repeat

—or—

<u>Step 2b</u>
Length + 16" ÷ pattern repeat = number of repeats required (round upward to nearest whole number)

<u>Step 2c</u>
Number of repeats required x pattern repeat = cut length

<u>Step 2d</u>
Number of widths x cut length ÷ 36 = yardage with pattern repeat

Work Order Specifications:

1. Width
2. Length
3. Inside or outside mount
4. Color of lining
5. Details of banding (if applicable)

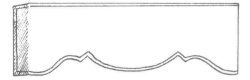

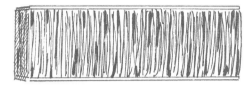

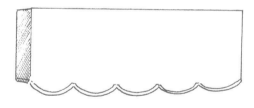

Description:
Upholstered cornices provide a classic topping for windows of any size, making an excellent overtreatment from draperies, vertical blinds or Venetian blinds. The cornice is constructed of a wooden frame that is padded and upholstered in a decorative fabric and finished with piping on the top and bottom edges.

Yardage:
See adjacent box (this page, below)

Work Order Specifications:
1. Width
2. Length: shortest + longest points
3. Return
4. Style
5. Fabric details
6. Color of lining

Special Note:
1. A check measure and installation are strongly recommended.
2. Off center prints may create an unbalanced effect, so choose fabric carefully.

Style	Width		
	48" to 84"	84" to 120"	120" to 144"
Tailored	2 yards	3 yards	3½ yards
Square Notch	2 yards	3 yards	3½ yards
Scallop	2 yards	3 yards	3½ yards
Scroll	2 yards	3 yards	3½ yards
Ruched	3 yards	4½ yards	5½ yards

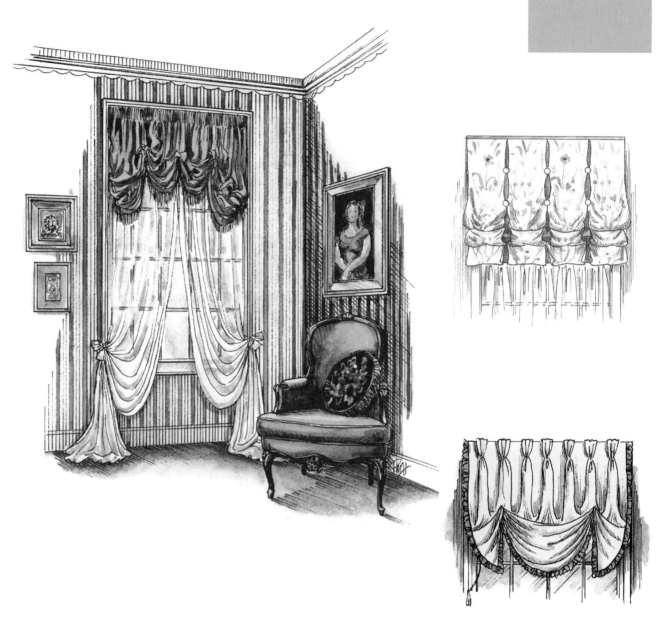

F ROM VICTORIAN TO ART DECO to modern, fabric shades are a fitting contribution to almost every decorating style. Their simplicity allows them to accompany other window treatments while their classic lines allow them to individually grace a window. For an especially appropriate choice, a fabric shade can be a splendid addition to oddly shaped windows, such as a bay or bow. In a child's room, a fabric shade will ensure rooms are dark and cozy, and in kitchens, their lack of interlining will keep odors from lingering in the fabric.

To determine the shade that suits your interior best, consider each style, as well as its lifting mechanisms, carefully. For example, Austrian shades are gathered both horizontally and vertically for a full look. When lowered, they offer the swagged effect of a curtain, and when raised appear much like a valance.

Roman shades present a more modern silhouette. With their bold lines and clean, tailored edges, this type of shade makes an attractive solitary window treatment. Its simplicity is also complementary to a more dramatic drapery or valance. Roller shades are economical, practical and simple to use. Often, the leading edge of the shade is embellished with fringe, pull tassels and other pretty details. So many choices!

Austrian shade under swags and cascades

Pleated cloud shade

Balloon shade with ruffles under cornice box

Arched cloud shade with bows

Arched balloon shade with ruffles on the bottom

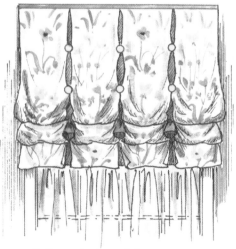

Balloon shade with button accents

Austrian shade with coordinated ruffle

Cathedral A-frame cloud shade

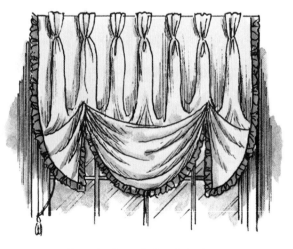

French pleated cloud shade

Roman shade on decorative rod

Roman shade with fan bottom

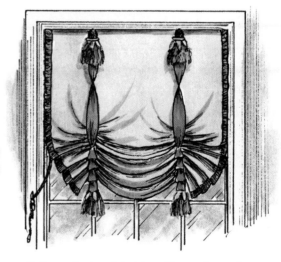

Balloon shade with side ruffles and tassels

Balloon shade with bullion fringe bottom

Scalloped heading cloud shade

Flat Roman shade with ties

Cloud shade under cloud valance

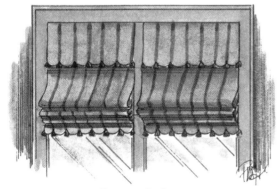

Roman shades

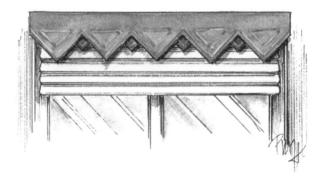

Roman shade with triangle valance

Balloon shade

Balloon shade under chevron valance

Cloud shade on decorative rod

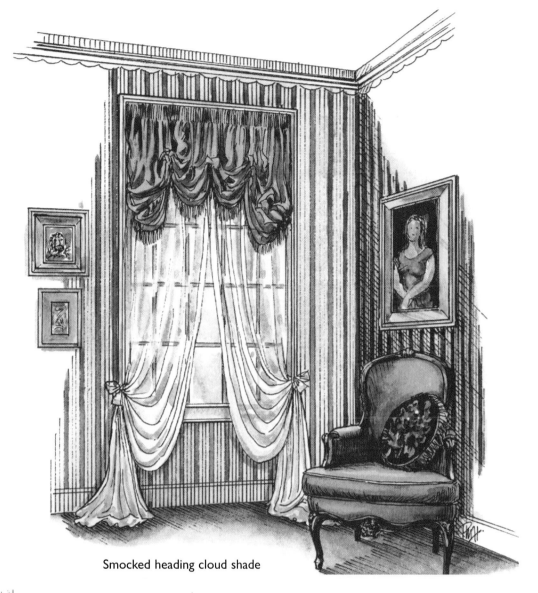

Smocked heading cloud shade

Roman shade under valance

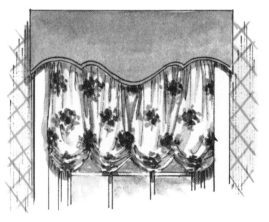

Cloud shade under cornice box

Stagecoach shade with ties

Wide pleated balloon shade

Designer cloud shade

Wide cloud shade

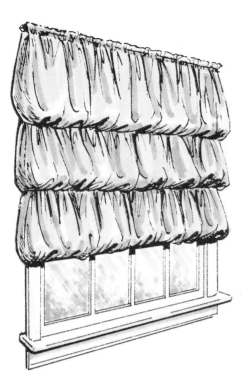

Tiered cloud shade

Cloud shade with ruffled bottom

Arched top cloud shade

Bottom arched balloon shade

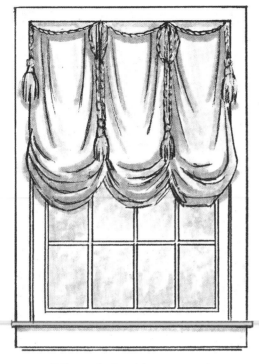

Balloon shade with rope tassels

Suspender balloon shade

Double rod pocket cloud shade
with bottom ruffle

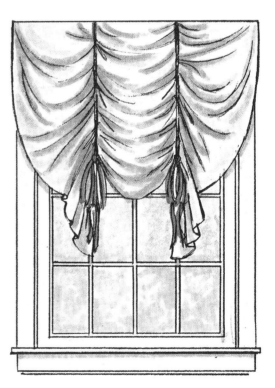

Specialty soft shade

Cloud shade with bows at top

Cloud shade gathered on a pole
with ruffled upper edge

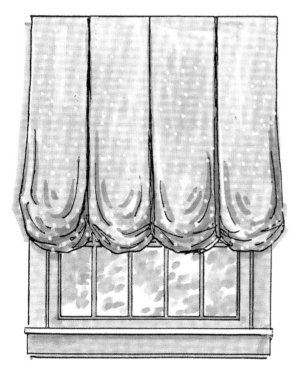

Traditional balloon shade

Balloon shade with shirred cornice box

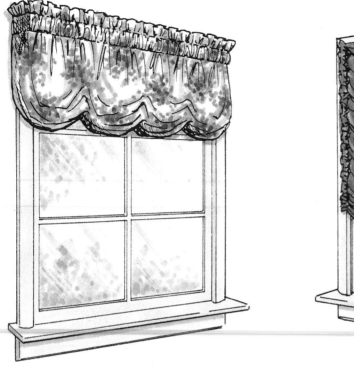

Cloud shade gathered on a pole with ruffle
at the top

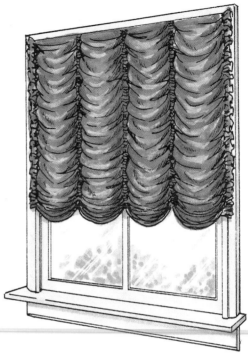

Triple fullness Austrian shade with
scalloped panels

Cloud shade with four-inch shirring

Shirred cloud shade with matching valance

Balloon shade with inverted pleats and
pouffed bottom edge

Pleated balloon shade with
matching valance

Triple fullness shade gathered on
horizontal rods

Rod pocket swagged balloon
shade over mini blind

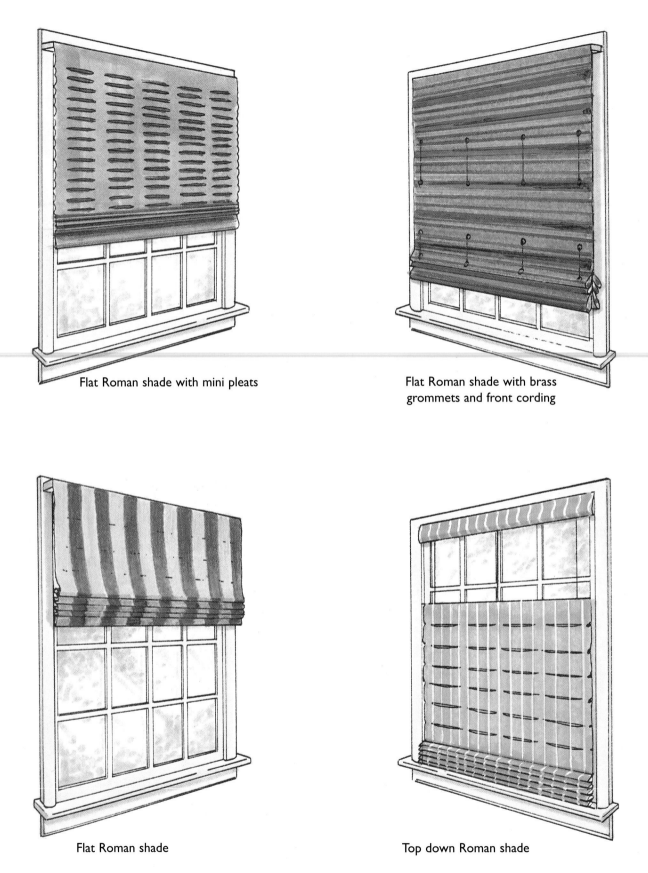

Flat Roman shade with mini pleats

Flat Roman shade with brass grommets and front cording

Flat Roman shade

Top down Roman shade

Flat fold Roman
shade with
horizontal pleats

Roman
shade with
mini pleats

Roman shade with overlapping folds

Roman shade with alternating
large and small pleats

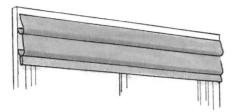

Soft Fold Roman valance with no returns

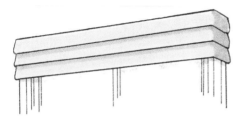

Wrapped Roman fold valance

Soft mini fold Roman shade

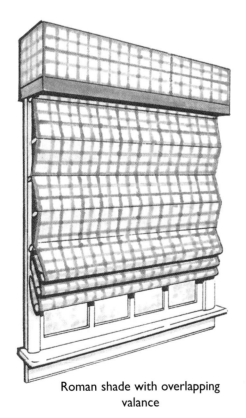

Roman shade with overlapping
valance

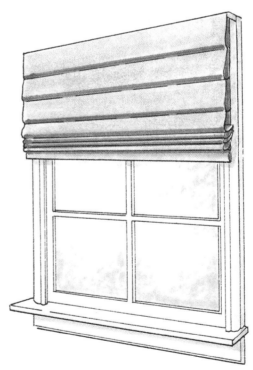

Flat fold Roman shade

CLOUD SHADES

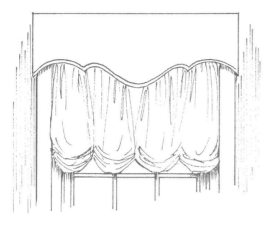

Description:
A fully functional shade with a gathered heading that falls into soft poufs that can be finished with or without a skirt.

Yardage:
Step 1:
Width of window ÷ returns x 2.5 ÷ width of fabric = number of widths (whole numbers only)

Step 2A
Number of widths x (length of shade + 20") ÷ 36 = yardage without pattern repeat

—or—

Step 2B:
Length of shade ÷ 20" ÷ pattern repeat = number of repeats required (round upward to nearest whole number)

Step 2C:
Number of repeats required x pattern repeat = cut length

Step 2D:
Number of widths x cut length ÷ 36 = yardage with pattern repeat

Work Order Specifications:
1. Width
2. Length
3. Color of lining
4. Inside or outside mount
5. Skirt or no skirt
6. Size of returns or size of board
7. Ceiling or wall mount
8. Right or left pull

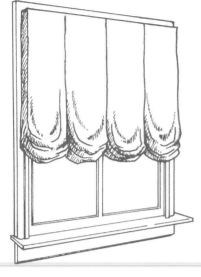

Description:
A fully functional shade with large inverted pleats for a more tailored look that is softened by billowing poufs.

Yardage:

Step 1:
Width of window ÷ returns x 3 ÷ width of fabric = number of widths (whole numbers only)

Step 2A:
Number of widths x (length of shade ÷ 20) ÷ 36 = yardage without pattern repeat

—or—

Step 2B:
Length of shade + 20" ÷ pattern repeat = number of repeats required (round upward to nearest whole number)

Step 2C:
Number of repeats required x pattern repeat = cut length

Step 2D:
Number of widths x cut length ÷ 36 = yardage with pattern repeat

Work Order Specifications:
1. Width
2. Length
3. Color of lining
4. Inside or outside mount
5. Skirt or no skirt
6. Size of returns or size of board
7. Ceiling or wall mount
8. Right or left pull

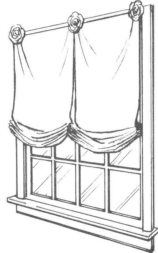

Specifications

Description:
A versatile shade that hangs straight and collapses into folds as it is raised. The Roman shade fits many different décors, from contemporary to traditional to formal. To add interest to the shade, use contrast bands, a scalloped edge or a single permanent pleat at the bottom.

Step 1:
Width of area to be covered x 5" ÷ width of fabric = number of widths (whole numbers only)

Step 2A:
Number of widths x (length of area + 12") ÷ 36 = yardage without pattern repeat

—or—

Step 2B:
Length of window + 12" ÷ pattern repeat = number of repeats required (round upward to nearest whole number)

Step 2C:
Number of repeats required x pattern repeat = cut length

Step 2D:
Number of widths x cut length ÷ 36 = yardage with pattern repeat

Work Order Specifications:
1. Width
2. Length
3. Color of lining
4. Inside or outside mount
5. Right or left pull

Special Note:
1. Roman shades are not recommended wider or longer than 84".
2. Cannot be made with returns.

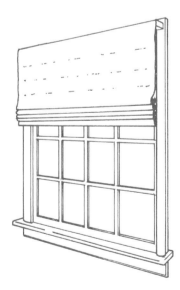

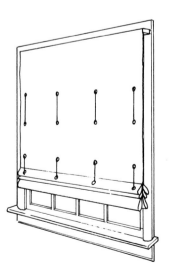

FOLDED ROMAN SHADES

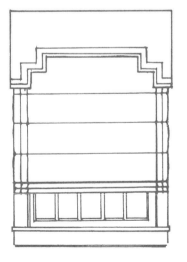

Description:
A folded Roman shade is designed with overlapping folds cascading down the full length of the shade.

Yardage:
Step 1:
Width of window + 5" ÷ width of fabric = number of widths (whole numbers only)

Step 2A:
Number of widths x (length of area x 2.5) ÷ 36 = yardage without pattern repeat

—or—

Step 2B:
Length of window x 2.5 ÷ pattern repeat = number of repeats required (round upward to nearest whole number)

Step 2C:
Number of repeats required x pattern repeat = cut length

Step 2D:
Number of widths x cut length ÷ 36 = yardage with pattern repeat

Work Order Specifications:
1. Width
2. Length
3. Color of lining
4. Inside or outside mount
5. Right or left pull

Special Note:
1. Folded Roman shades larger than 60" in width or 84" in length are not recommended.
2. Due to the nature of the fabric, the folds do not hang evenly, therefore they are not recommended for an application where two or more blinds are side by side.
3. Cannot be made with returns.

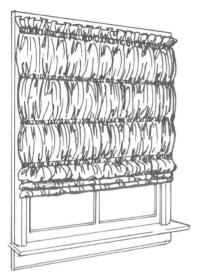

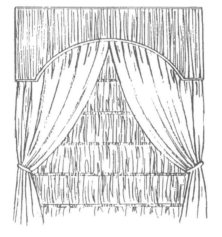

Specifications

Description:

Fabric is shirred onto rods to create this very elegant yet functional shade that adds romance to the look of a traditional Roman shade.

Yardage:

Step 1:

Width of window x 3 ÷ width of fabric = number of widths (whole numbers only)

Step 2A:

Length of window x 1.25 x number of widths ÷ 36 = yardage without pattern repeat

—or—

Step 2B:

Length of window x 1.25 ÷ pattern repeat = number of repeats required (round upward to nearest whole number)

Step 2C:

Number of repeats required x pattern repeat = cut length

Step 2D:

Number of widths x cut length ÷ 36 = yardage with pattern repeat

Work Order Specifications:

1. Width
2. Length
3. Right or left cord pull
4. Inside or outside mount
5. Lining color (if applicable)

Special Note:

1. Use only soft, drapeable fabrics for optimum effect.
2. This treatment cannot be made with returns and therefore is intended to be used alone or as an undertreatment.
3. Not recommended wider than 60".

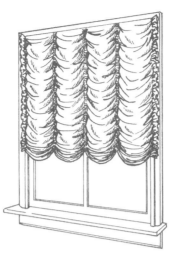

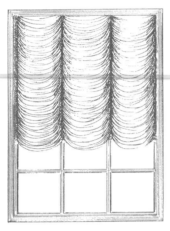

Specifications

Description:
A soft, formal treatment created by vertical shirring between scallops.

Yardage:
Step 1:
(Width of area to be covered x 1.5) ÷ width of fabric = number of widths (whole numbers only)
Step 2A:
Number of widths x (length of area x 3) ÷ 36 = yardage without pattern repeat
—or—
Step 2B:
Length of area x 3 ÷ pattern repeat = number of repeats required (round upward to nearest whole number)
Step 2C:
Number of repeats required x pattern repeat = cut length
Step 2D:
Number of widths x cut length ÷ 36 = yardage with pattern repeat

Work Order Specifications:
1. Width
2. Length
3. Color of lining (if applicable)
4. Inside or outside mount
5. Right or left cord pull

Special Note:
1. This treatment has a tendency to pull in on the sides. It should not be used where this will cause a problem.
2. Use heavier fabric for privacy or sheer or lace fabric for a more decorative look.
3. It can be used as a single treatment or in combination with draperies or valances.

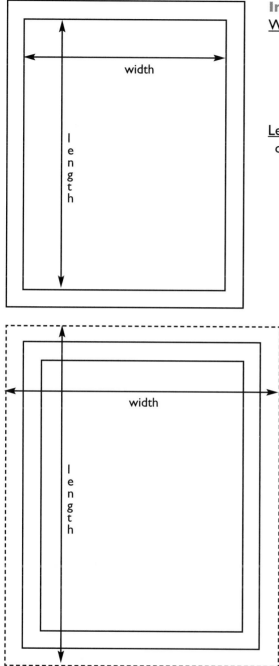

Inside or Recessed Mount:

<u>Width:</u> Measure width of window at the top, center and bottom of window. Use the narrowest measurement when ordering. Specify on order form if outside clearance has been made. If no clearance has been allowed, the factory will deduct ¼" from the overall width.

<u>Length:</u> Measure the height of the window from top of opening to top of sill, no allowance is made for length.

Outside or Wall Mount:

<u>Width:</u> Measure exact width of the area to be covered. It is recommended that shades extend past actual window opening by two inches on each side. Furnish finished shade width, no allowances will be made.

<u>Length:</u> Measure length of area to be covered, allowing a minimum of 2½" at top of window to accommodate headerboard and brackets. At this time you may want to take into consideration stackage of shades and allow for this in your length measurement. Furnish finished shade length, no allowance will be made.

All Installations

- Specify right or left cord position. If no cord position is indicated, cords will be corded to right hand side.
- Specify cord length (length of cord needed for easy reach, when shade is completely down). If no specification is made, cord will be approximately one-third the length of the shade.
- For pole cloud, cloud and balloon shades, specify if length given is high or low point of pouf.

Fabric Shade Square Footage Chart

Square Footage Chart

Shade Length in inches (rows) × Shade Width in inches (columns)

Length \ Width	24	30	36	42	48	54	60	66	72	78	84	90	96	102	108	114	120	126	132	138	144
30	10	10	10	10	10	11¼	12½	13¾	15	16¼	17½	18¾	20	21¼	22½	23¾	25	26¼	27½	28¾	30
36	10	10	10	10½	12	13½	15	16½	18	19½	21	22½	24	25½	27	28½	30	31½	33	34½	36
42	10	10	10½	12¼	14	15¾	17½	19¼	21	22¾	24½	26¼	28	29¾	31½	33¼	35	36¾	38½	40¼	42
48	10	10	12	14	16	18	20	22	24	26	28	30	32	34	36	38	40	42	44	46	48
54	10	11¼	13½	15¾	18	20¼	22½	24¾	27	29¼	31½	33¾	36	38¼	40½	42¾	45	47¼	49½	51¾	54
60	10	12½	15	17½	20	22½	25	27½	30	32½	35	37½	40	42½	45	47½	50	52½	55	57½	60
66	11	13¾	16½	19¼	22	24¾	27½	30¼	33	35¾	38½	41¼	44	46¾	49½	52¼	55	57¾	60½	63¼	66
72	12	15	18	21	24	27	30	33	36	39	42	45	48	51	54	57	60	63	66	69	72
78	13	16¼	19½	22¾	26	29¼	32½	35¾	39	42¼	45½	48¾	52	55¼	58½	61¾	65	68¼	71½	74¾	78
84	14	17½	21	24½	28	31½	35	38½	42	45½	49	52½	56	59½	63	66½	70	73½	77	80½	84
90	15	18¾	22½	26¼	30	33¾	37½	41¼	45	48¾	52½	56¼	60	63¾	67½	71¼	75	78¾	82½	86¼	90
96	16	20	24	28	32	36	40	44	48	52	56	60	64	68	72	76	80	84	88	92	96
102	17	21¼	25½	29¾	34	38¼	42½	46¾	51	55¼	59½	63¾	68	72¼	76½	80¾	85	89¼	93½	97¾	102
108	18	22½	27	31½	36	40½	45	49½	54	58½	63	67½	72	76½	81	85½	90	94½	99	103½	108
114	19	23¾	28½	33¼	38	42¾	47½	52¼	57	61¾	66½	71¼	76	80¾	85½	90¼	95	99¾	104½	109¼	114
120	20	25	30	35	40	45	50	55	60	65	70	75	80	85	90	95	100	105	110	115	120
126	21	26¼	31½	36¾	42	47¼	52½	57¾	63	68¼	73½	78¾	84	89¼	94½	99¾	105	110¼	115½	120¾	126
132	22	27½	33	38½	44	49½	55	60½	66	71½	77	82½	88	93½	99	104½	110	115½	121	126½	132
138	23	28¾	34½	40¼	46	51¾	57½	63¼	69	74¾	80½	86¼	92	97¾	103½	109¼	115	120¾	126½	132¼	138
144	24	30	36	42	48	54	60	66	72	78	84	90	96	102	108	114	120	126	132	138	144

©1986 Carol's Roman Shades

N O MATTER HOW WELL DONE A ROOM, it is in the details that individuality and personal expression emerge. One can tie back a drapery—but have you considered how many different ways there are to accomplish this task? Ruffles, bows, simple bands, rosettes, jewels—these are some of the many methods to pull back cloth from a window. Consider your sofa. Would the addition of an eye-catching throw pillow or two dress up the room? How about an alpaca wool blanket, draped over the sofa's arm, in the winter months?

Consider room dividers, slipcovers, lamp shades and table linens such as placemats, napkins, tablecloths and napkin rings. How might you employ these accessories to make your space speak of the people who live in your home? How can these items change out depending upon the season? Will the simple change of silk flowers and vase on your dining room table celebrate an impending holiday with style?

Various bed crowns

Rod pocket drapery with decorative rod
over plain bedspread

Swags and cascades over floral bedspread
with upholstered headboard

Swags and jabots with Maltese Cross ties
over plain bedspread

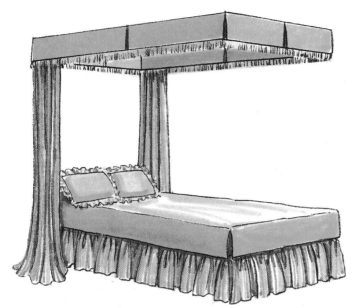

Ceiling mounted valance over box pleated coverlet

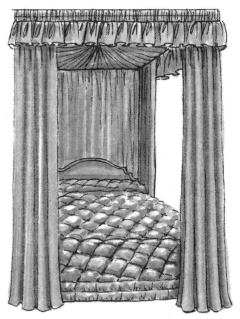

Ceiling mounted rod pocket valance over
quilted bedspread

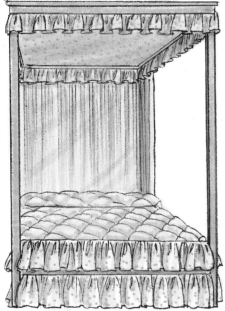

Quilted top double ruffled
drop bedspread

Plain bedspread with side panels

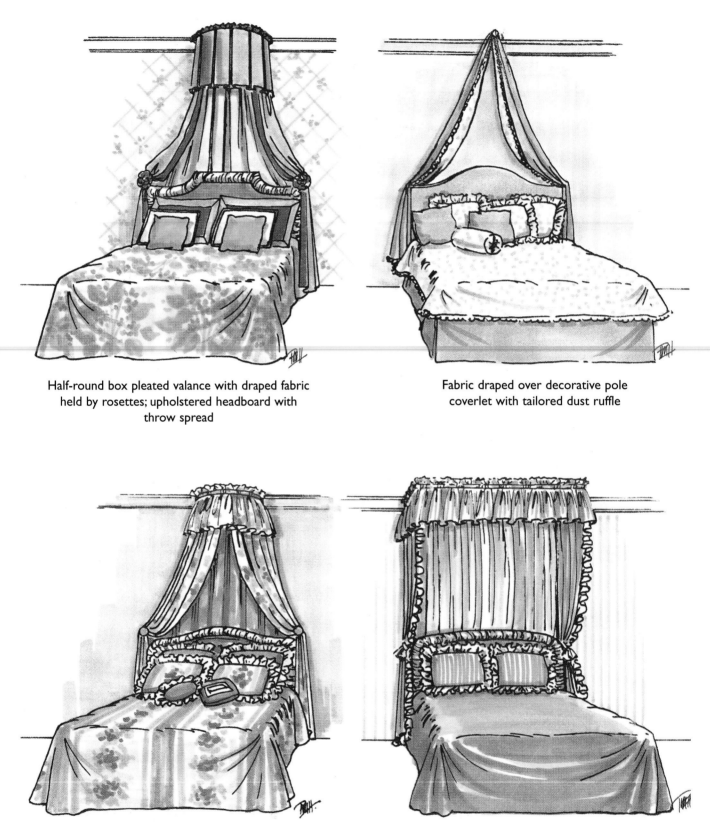

Half-round box pleated valance with draped fabric
held by rosettes; upholstered headboard with
throw spread

Fabric draped over decorative pole
coverlet with tailored dust ruffle

Half-round ruffled valance with fabric draped over
hold backs; upholstered headboard with throw spread

Rod pocket valance with ruffled tiebacks;
upholstered headboard and throw spread

Box pleated canopy valance with stationary draperies;
quilted coverlet over box pleated dust ruffle

Gathered canopy valance; ruffled bedspread
over gathered dust ruffle

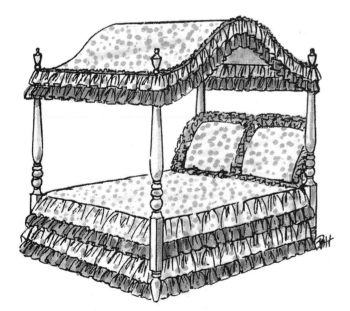

Arched canopy with ruffles; ruffled bedspread
and dust ruffle

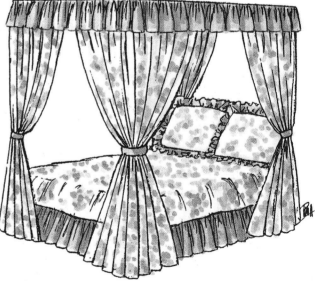

Gathered canopy valance over tiebacks; coverlet over
gathered dust ruffle

BEDSPREADS & UPHOLSTERED BENCHES

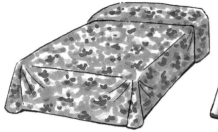

Throw spread

Throw with scalloped edge

Fitted throw

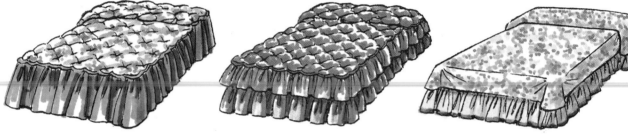

Scalloped quilted top with shirred drop

Scalloped quilted top with double shirred drop

Throw with ruffled bottom

Plain coverlet over shirred dust ruffle

Quilted coverlet over shirred dust ruffle

Throw with 1" welt

Throw with 2" welt

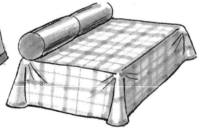

Studio couch cover with bolsters

Tufted daybed comforter over shirred dust ruffle

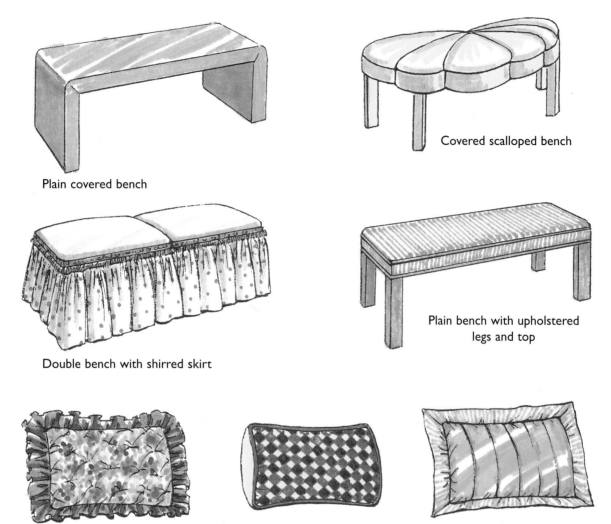

Plain covered bench

Covered scalloped bench

Double bench with shirred skirt

Plain bench with upholstered legs and top

Sham with 3" ruffle

Plain sham with ¼" welt

Quilted sham with 2½" flange

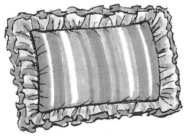

Plain sham with double ruffle

Sham with ¼" welt and ruffle

Double ruffle sham with ½" welt

Cylindrical bolster with welt trim

Wedge bolster with welt trim

Rectangular bolster with welt trim

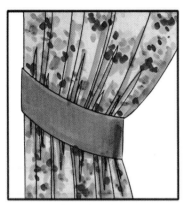

Straight plain

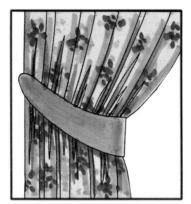

Tapered plain

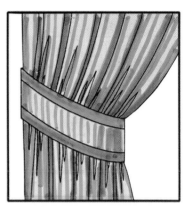

Straight with banding

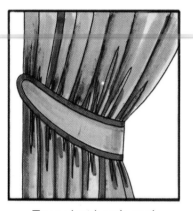

Tapered with welt cord

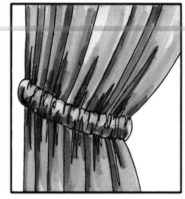

Shirred jumbo welt cord

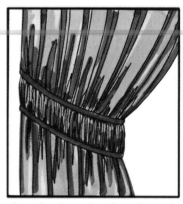

Straight shirred with welt cord

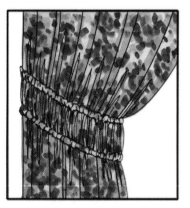

Straight shirred

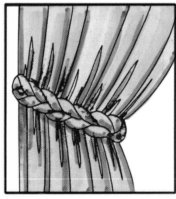

Braided

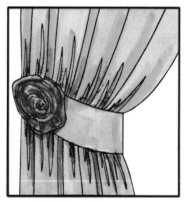

Straight with rosette

Straight with bow

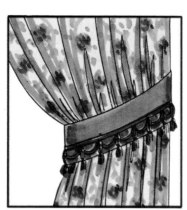

Straight with fringe

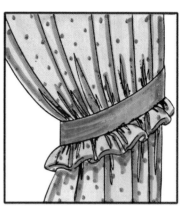

Straight with ruffle

Ruffled

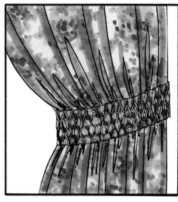

New shirred look

Formal tie with cascade

Shirred tie with pleat

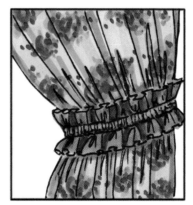

Double ruffled tie

Box pleated tie with welt

Placemats

Seat cushions

Lamp shades

Rosettes

Napkins & napkin rings

Bows

Round ottoman

Square ottoman

Fabric draped vanity table

Slip-covered chair

Placemats

Fabric draped through
sconces

Fabric covered
wastebasket

Seat cushion

Sconces

ROUND TABLE COVERS & UNUSUAL FABRIC SHIRRING

Ruffled overlay and skirt with tassels

Round overlay tied with bows

Plain round cover: lined or unlined

Plain round cover with welt edge

lace square over skirt

Round cover with Austrian shirring

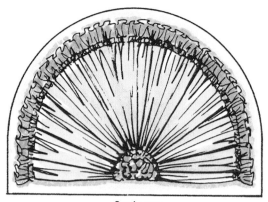

Sunburst

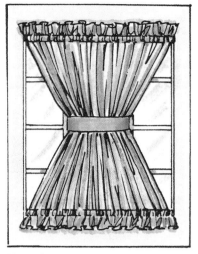

Hourglass rod top and bottom

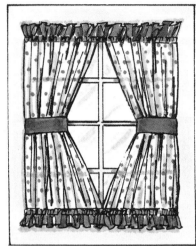

Diamond rod top and bottom

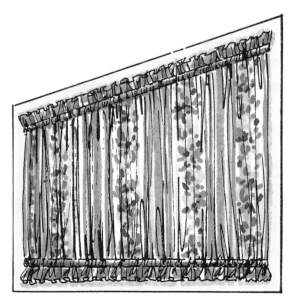

Slant rod top and bottom

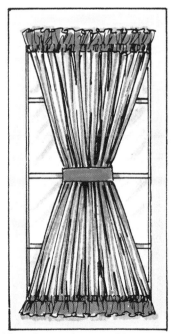

Hourglass rod top and bottom

Turkish corners

Knife edge with ¼" welt

3" ruffle with welt

Heart shaped with ruffle

Shirred welt

Square knot

Round pillow with welt & ruffle

Round pillow with plain welt & button

Round pillow with plain welt & button

Rope welt on knife edge

Scalloped ruffle with welt edge

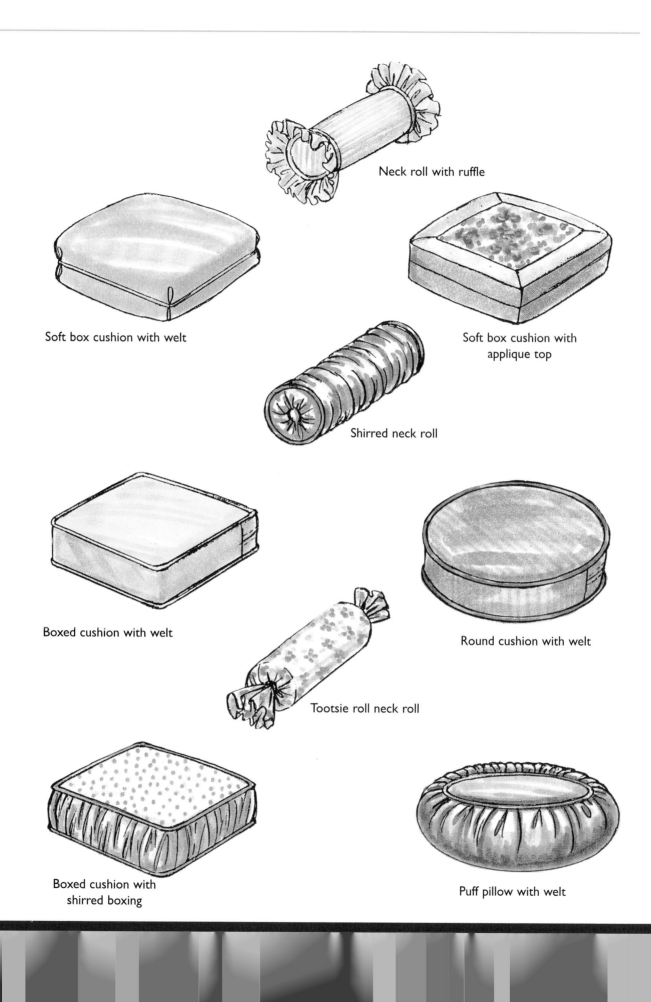

Neck roll with ruffle

Soft box cushion with welt

Soft box cushion with applique top

Shirred neck roll

Boxed cushion with welt

Tootsie roll neck roll

Round cushion with welt

Boxed cushion with shirred boxing

Puff pillow with welt

DUSTERS

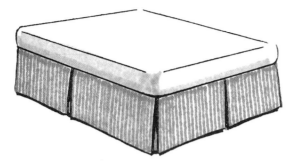

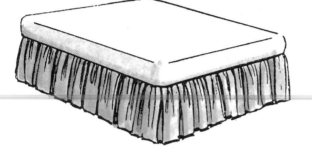

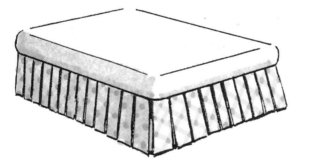

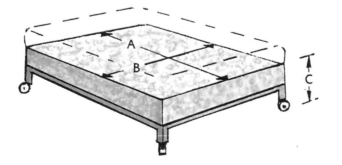

Description—Dusters:

A duster, which fits in between the mattress and the boxspring, is a clever way to not only provide your bed with a finished appearance, effectively hiding the more unsightly but necessary box spring, but also covers the distance between the boxspring and the floor. There are three popular styles: straight tailored, shirred (or ruffled) and box pleated.

How to Measure:

Exact measurements are necessary.

A. Measure the length of the boxspring
B. Measure the width of the boxspring
C. Measure the drop from the top of the boxspring to the floor

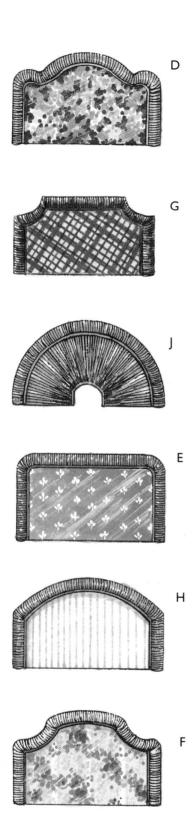

D

G

J

E

H

F

Specifications

Description—Upholstered Headboard:

Sumptuous and luxurious, the upholstered headboard is not only stylish but also offers extreme comfort for those individuals who like to read in bed, yet loathe leaning against a wood or iron headboard. Plus, the shape of the headboard and the colors and fabric patterns make headboards perfect for those who want to exhibit individual style in their most private home area.

Dimensions:

Style D, I, F, & G:
 Twin = 41" wide x 51" high
 Full = 56" wide x 53" high
 Queen = 62" w x 55" high
 King = 81" wide x 56" high

Style J:
 Twin = 41" wide x 53" high
 Full = 56" wide x 55" high
 Queen = 62" w x 57" high
 King = 81" wide x 57" high

Style E & H:
 Twin = 41" wide x 49" high
 Full = 56" wide x 49" high
 Queen = 62" w x 51" high
 King = 81" wide x 53" high

SPREADS & UPHOLSTERED BENCHES

Spreads

	36"	48"	54"
Twin	12 yards	8 yards	8 yards
Full	12 yards	12 yards	8 yards
Queen	15 yards	12 yards	12 yards
King	15 yards	12 yards	12 yards

Additional yardage requirements:
For prints—Add 1 yard
Additional Yardage Optional features:
For reverse sham—add 3 yards; For jumbo cord—add 2 yards

Comforter Yardage

Twin, Full, Queen = 7 yards/side
King = 11 yards/side

Pillow Shams

1½ yards; Ruffles, add 1½ yards

Bolsters

	36"	45"	54"
36"	1½ yards	1½ yards	1 yards
39"	2 yards	1½ yards	1 yards
60"	2 yards	2 yards	2 yards
72"	2½ yards	2 yards	2 yards

Add 1 repeat of pattern for prints

Dusters

	36" Fabric		45" or Wider	
	Tailored	**Shirred or 4" Box Pleat**	**Tailored**	**Shirred or 4" Box Pleat**
Twin	3¾ yards	8½ yards	2¾ yards	6½ yards
Full	3¾ yards	8½ yards	2¾ yards	7 yards
Queen	4½ yards	10 yards	3 yards	7½ yards
King	4½ yards	10 yards	3 yards	7½ yards

General Information

Bedspreads are made to fit the following standard bed sizes: Twin: 39 x 75; Full: 54 x 75; Queen: 60 x 80; King: 72 x 84. Standard drops: Bedspread: 21"; Coverlet: 12"; Duster: 14"; Pillow tuck: 15"

TABLE LINENS

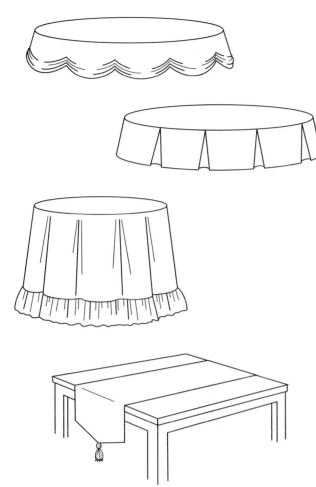

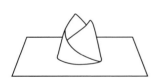

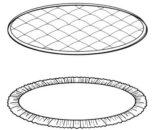

Description—Tablecloths & Toppers:

Decorative tablecloths and toppers can complement any room décor. The tablecloth is finished with piping at the bottom and may have jumbo piping, ruched or ruffles added. Table toppers complete the look in a basic square handkerchief, stylish Austrian or box pleated.

Yardage:
See chart below

Work Order Specifications:
1. Diameter of table
2. Drop measurement to the floor
3. Style of tablecloth or topper
4. Fabric details

Description—Napkins, Placemats and Runners:

Quilted placemats can be custom made to your color scheme and may be finished with piping or a one-inch ruffle. Coordinating 18" square dinner napkins are double hemmed and stitched. Runners add a decorative touch and display a fine wood or glass table to its best advantage.

Yardage:
Placemats:
  Print fabrics: 18–27" pattern repeat; allow 1 repeat per placemat
  Plain or small prints: allow 1/2 yard per placemat
  For ruffle, add 1/4 yard per placemat
Napkins
  Print fabrics: 18–27" pattern repeat
  1½ yards = 4 napkins
  Plain or small print: 1¼ yards = 4
Runners:
Length of table + 24" ÷ 36 = number of yards

Work Order Specifications:
1. Fabric details
2. Sizes

Yardage Chart

Round tablecloth with:	Up to 74" diameter	Up to 90" diameter
Regular piping	4¾ yards	6 yards
Jumbo piping	add 1½ yards	add 1½ yards
Ruched band	add 2½ yards	add 3 yards
Ruffle	add 4 yards	add 5 yards
Square handkerchief		
Topper (50")	1½ yards	1½ yards
Austrian topper	2¾ yards	3½ yards
Pleated topper	2¾ yards	3½ yards

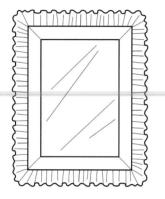

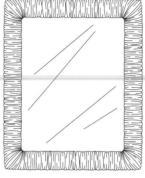

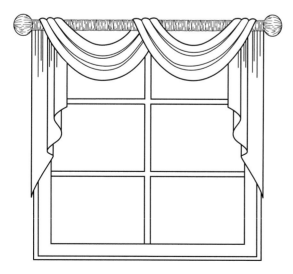

Specifications

Description—Upholstered Mirrors:
The ultimate in custom décor—fully upholstered mirrors. Fabric may be ruched onto a frame or pulled flat and finished around the edges with matching piping or ruffles.

Yardage:
Ruched:
 2 yards
Flat:
 1¼ yards
Piping:
 add 1/2 yard
Ruffle:
 add 11/4 yards

Work Order Specifications:
1. Style of mirror
2. Size of mirror
3. Fabric details

Description—Covered Rods:
For a truly customized window treatment, fabric-covered wood rods and finials add decorative flare. A swag casually draped over a rod or drapes on café rings are excellent ways in which this treatment can be used.

Yardage:
For rod and finial:
 Up to 60" wide: allow 1 yard
 Up to 108" wide: allow 1½ yards
 Up to 144" wide: allow 2 yards

Work Order Specifications:
1. Size and diameter of rod
2. Fabric details

SHOWER CURTAINS

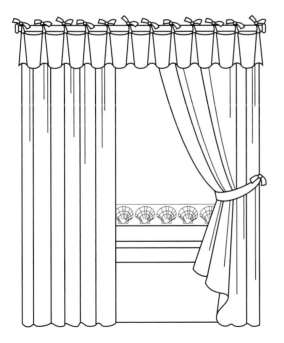

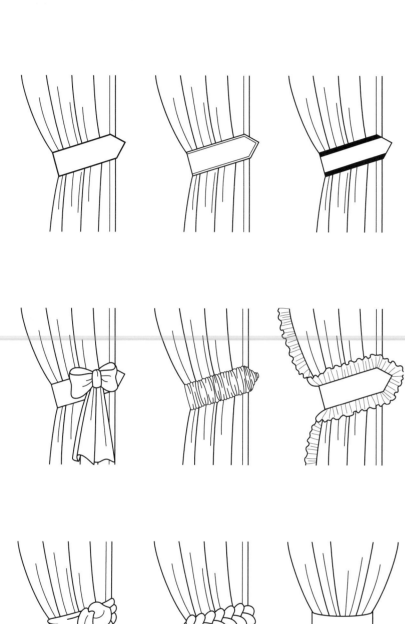

Specifications

Description:
A decorative accent by which draperies and curtains are held back from the window panes. The various styles give a personal touch to the window treatment.

Yardage:
Standard:
  1/2 yard
Standard with piping:
  1/2 yard + 1/2 yard piping
Standard with banding:
  1/2 yard + 1/2 yard banding
Standard with bows:
  1/2 yard + 1 yard bows
Contour:
  3/4 yard
Ruched tieback:
  1 yard
Ruffled tieback:
  1 yard + 1½ yard ruffle
Streamer tieback:
  2 yards
Braided tieback:
  1/2 yard each strand (three strands)
Collar with hook and loop fastener:
  1/2 yard

Work Order Specifications:
1. Style
2. Fabric (if contrasts are used)

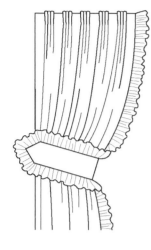

Specifications

Description:
There are many details that may be added to personalize a window treatment. Ruffles add charm and romance to the look of a room. Use on draperies, tiebacks, cushions or comforters for a country-style look.

Inset banding adds dramatic contrast to a window treatment. A band of two inches or more is sewn inset from the edges.

Reverse lining is a decorative facing sewn to the lining, then folded outward to reveal the contrast and held in place with tiebacks.

Fringe and braids used decoratively on a window treatment echo the elegance of past eras.

Yardage:
Ruffles:
 1/4 yard for each 24" ruffles
Inset banding:
 Length + hem allowances
Reverse lining:
 Length + hem allowances
Fringe and braids:
 Length + additional 10%

Work Order Specifications:
1. Treatment
2. Fabrics

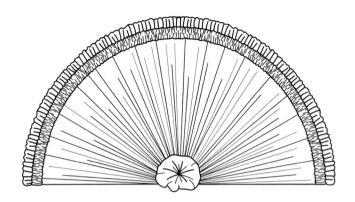

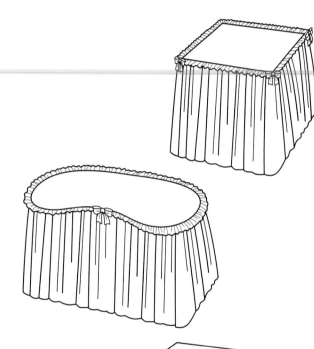

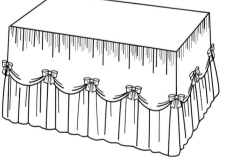

Specifications

Description—Sunburst:

A decorative accent for an arched window. The sunburst is softly gathered into the center and is usually made in a sheer or lace fabric to enhance (rather than block) the window and filter the light. A rosette may be added.

Yardage:

For 118" sheer or lace: 1½ yards
For 48" lace: 3½ yards
Windows up to 48" diameter

Work Order Specifications:

1. Specify fabric
2. Specify if a rosette is desired
3. A template of the window should be provided

Description—Dressing Tables & Stools:

A romantic detail to add to the most feminine bedroom. The separate cover is gathered in two styles, balloon or ruffled. Upholstered stools coordinate with either style.

Yardage:

Balloon style:
  Top and balloon skirt: 7 yards
  Underskirt: 5 yards
  Bows: 2 yards
Ruffled style:
  Skirt: 10 yards
  Contrast bow: 1/2 yard
Stool:
  Skirt: 3½ yards
  Bows: 1/2 yard (for two)

Work Order Specifications:

1. Style of table
2. Fabric details

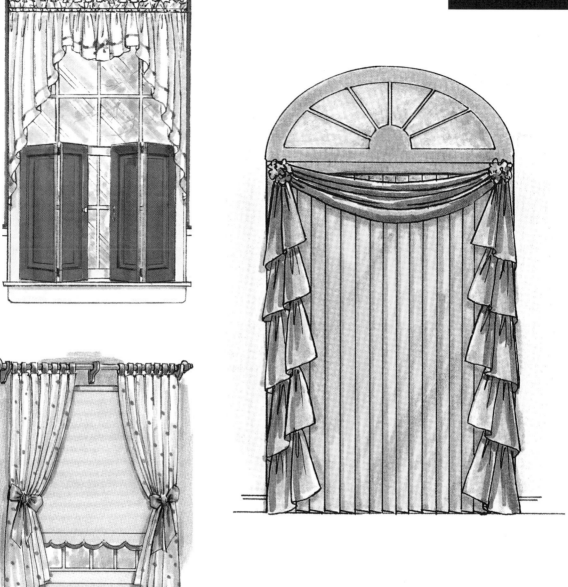

THIS BOOK HAS THUS FAR BEEN A CELEBRATION OF ALL THINGS FABRIC: draperies, fabric shades, curtains, valances. And yet, the practical good looks of a "hard" window treatment such as a blind or shutter need not be considered unimaginative. There are many charismatic options for those who prefer a more streamlined look at the window.

There are simple, vinyl roller shades for kitchen windows and woven wood shades that will beautifully complement a living room. There are stained wood Venetian blinds for the window above your desk and modest vertical blinds which fit nicely across sliding glass doors. Consider panel shutters for a bay window. No matter what type of hard window covering you decide upon, it is certain that your shades, blinds or shutters will fulfill your needs for visual impact and light control while they provide you with a calming sense of privacy.

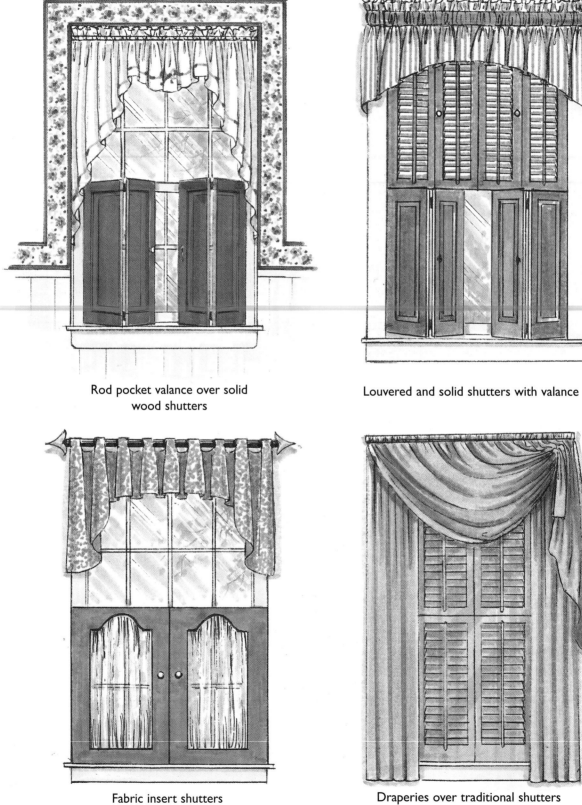

Rod pocket valance over solid
wood shutters

Louvered and solid shutters with valance

Fabric insert shutters

Draperies over traditional shutters

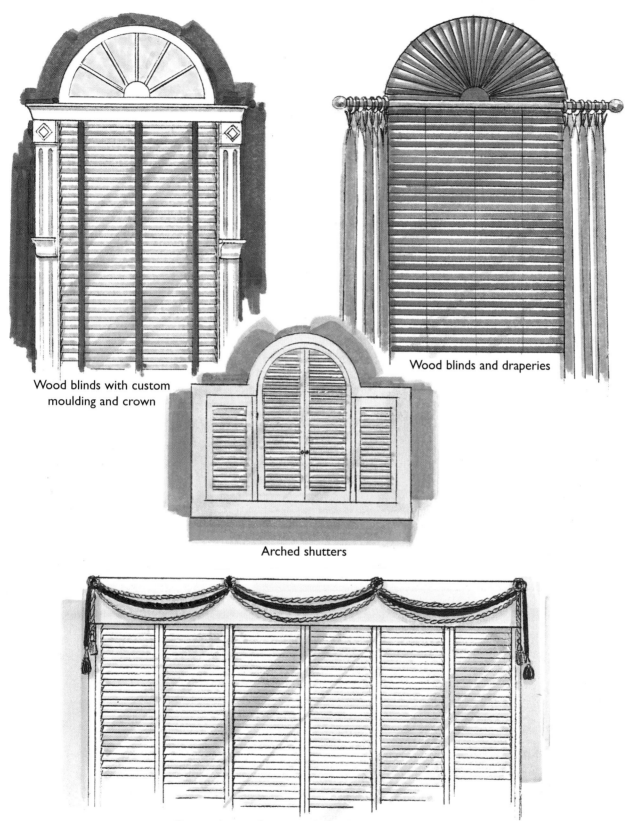

Wood blinds with custom
moulding and crown

Wood blinds and draperies

Arched shutters

Cornice box with rope and tassels over shutters

Fabric draped swag over blinds

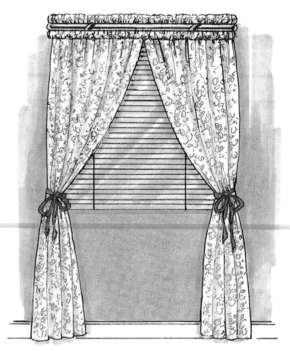

Lace tiebacks over wood blinds

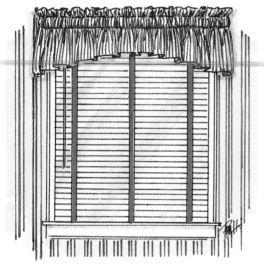

Arched gathered valance
over wood Venetian blinds

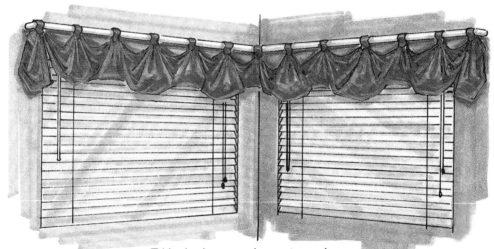

Tabbed valance on decorative rod
over wood blind

Swag and jabots over half shutters

Shirred valance with ruffle over
gathered side draperies and wood blind

Bishop sleeve arched valance
over Plantation shutters

Cloud valance over half shutters

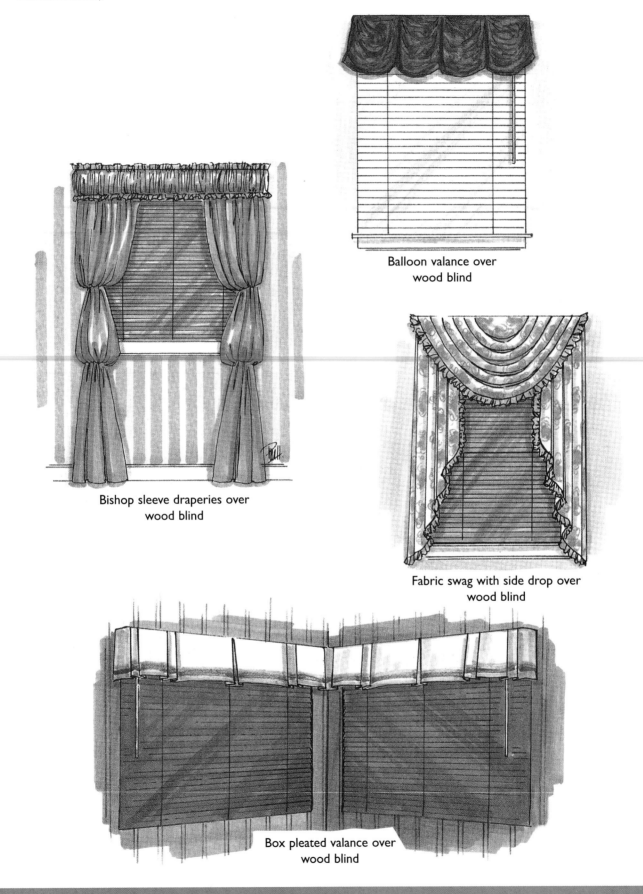

Balloon valance over
wood blind

Bishop sleeve draperies over
wood blind

Fabric swag with side drop over
wood blind

Box pleated valance over
wood blind

Ruffled swags over café shutters

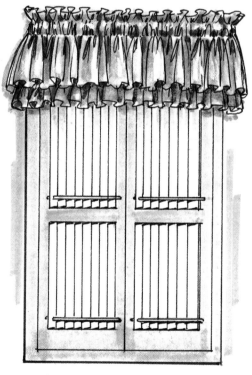

Two-tone swag over full shutters

Shutter with shirred fabric insert

Gathered valance over louvered
shutters

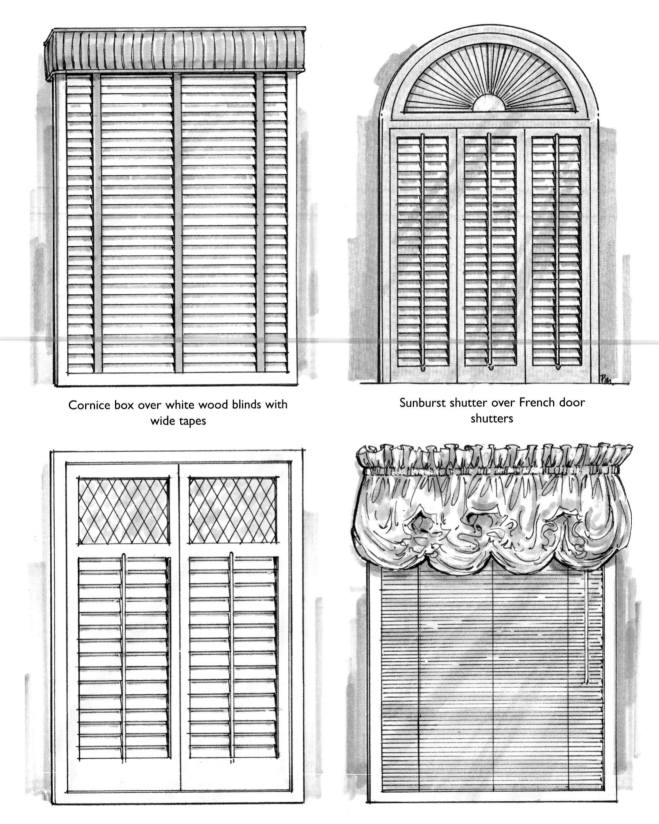

Cornice box over white wood blinds with
wide tapes

Sunburst shutter over French door
shutters

Leaded glass over wide blade shutters

One inch wood blind in natural finish with
cloud valance

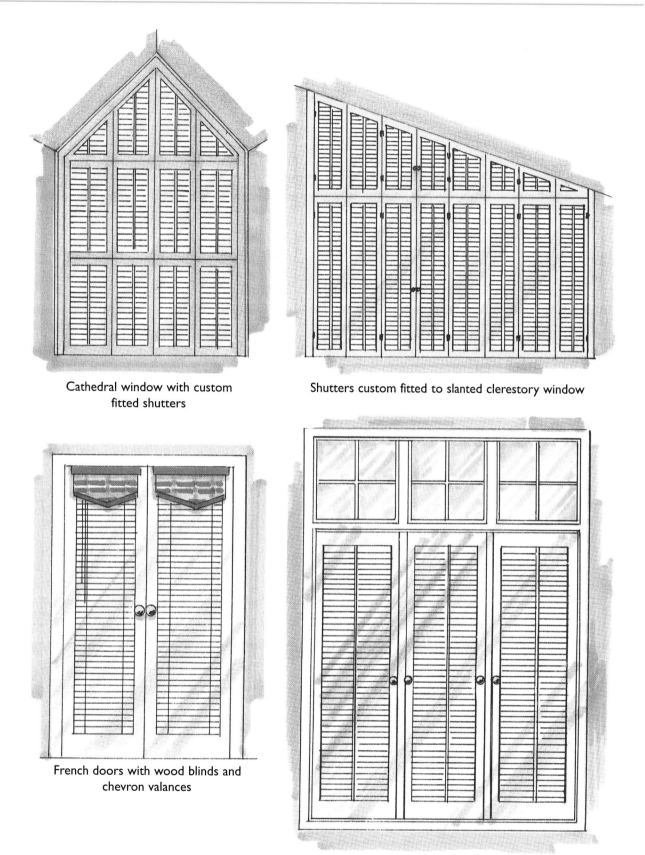

Cathedral window with custom
fitted shutters

Shutters custom fitted to slanted clerestory window

French doors with wood blinds and
chevron valances

Traditional shutters on tall window

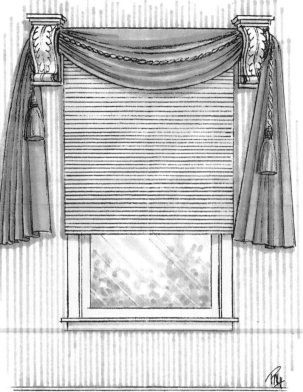

Drapery folded over decorative rod over
pleated shade

Fabric draped over pleated shade

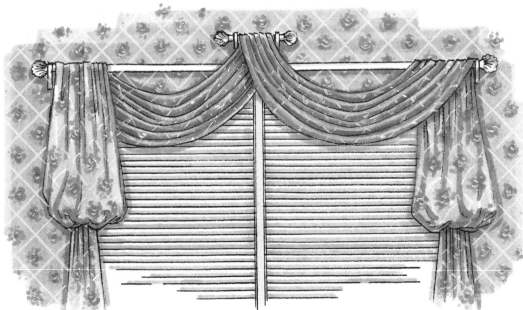

Fabric draped over pleated shade

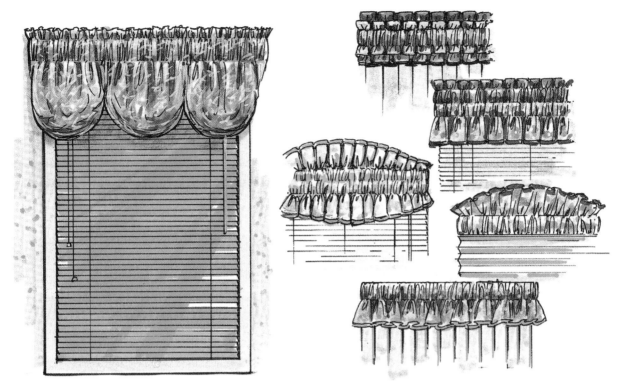

Cloud valance over mini blind

Alternate valance styles to accent blinds

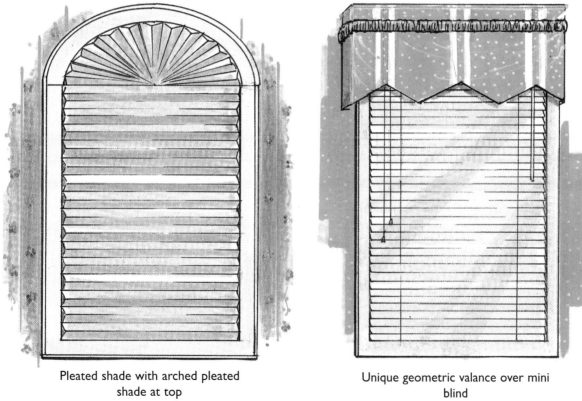

Pleated shade with arched pleated
shade at top

Unique geometric valance over mini
blind

Gathered valance with bows over shade
with appliqued bottom

Fringed scalloped roller shade with valance

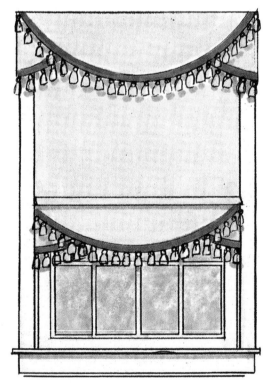

Banded roller shade with valance

Rod pocket valance over roller shade

Handkerchief tie over pleated blinds

Swag with tassels and fringe

Cloud shade with ruffled top and tassels

Short swag on decorative rod

Multiple lace fabric swags on decorative rod

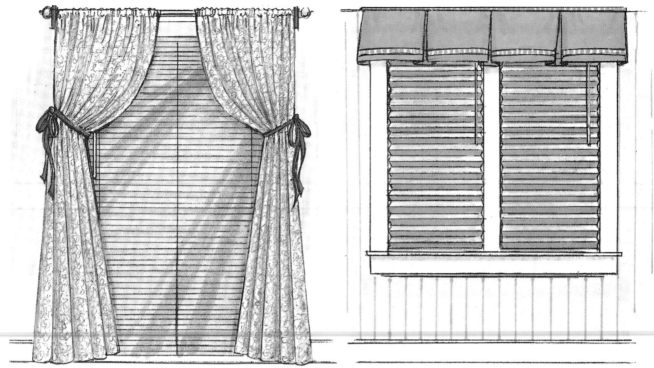

Lace tiebacks on decorative
rod over mini blind

Box pleated valance over pleated shade

Scalloped awning valance over mini blind

Full gathered valance on double rods

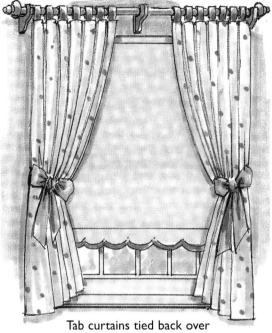

Tab curtains tied back over
roller shade

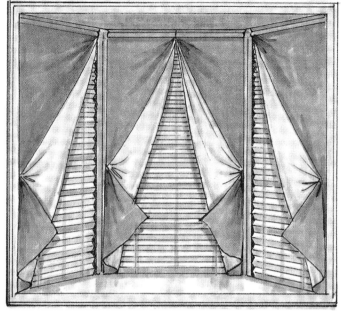

Flat panels pulled back over pleated shades

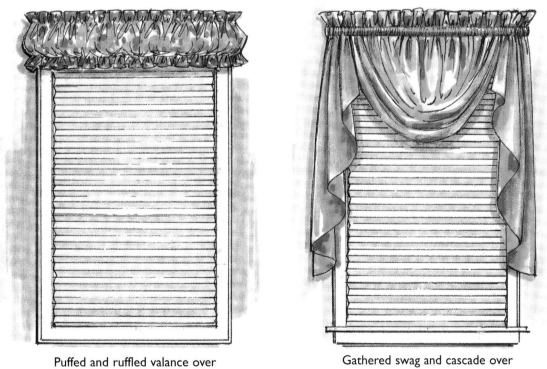

Puffed and ruffled valance over
pleated shade

Gathered swag and cascade over
pleated shade

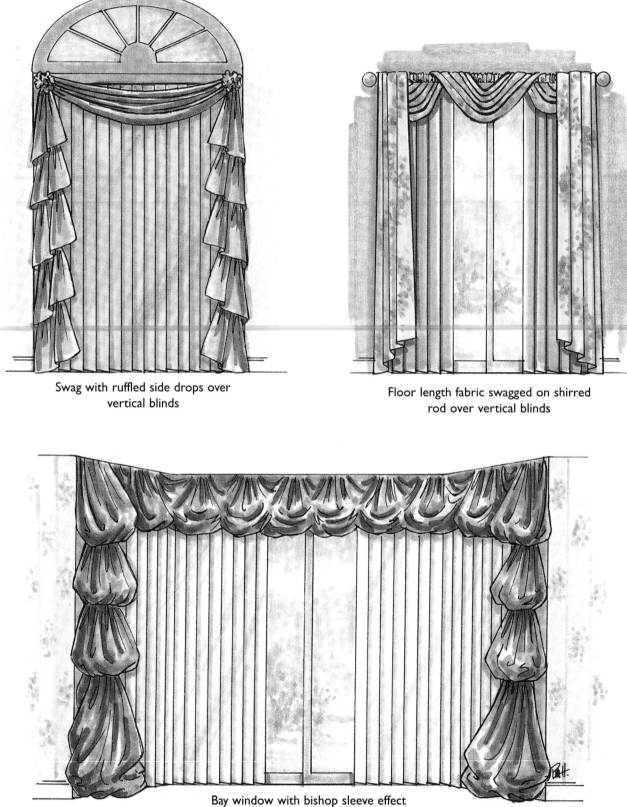

Swag with ruffled side drops over
vertical blinds

Floor length fabric swagged on shirred
rod over vertical blinds

Bay window with bishop sleeve effect
over vertical blinds

Simple shirred cornice over vertical blinds

Fabric or wallpaper inserts in
vertical blinds

Double gathered cornice over vertical blinds

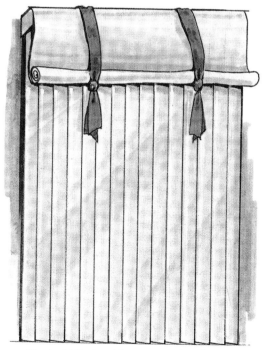

Vertical blinds with stagecoach valance

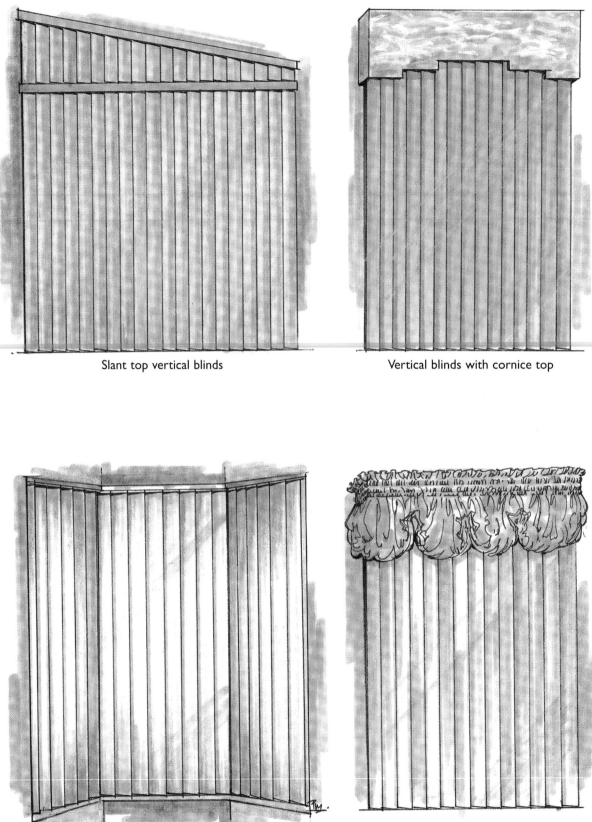

Slant top vertical blinds

Vertical blinds with cornice top

Vertical blinds in a bay window

Shirred cloud valance over vertical blinds

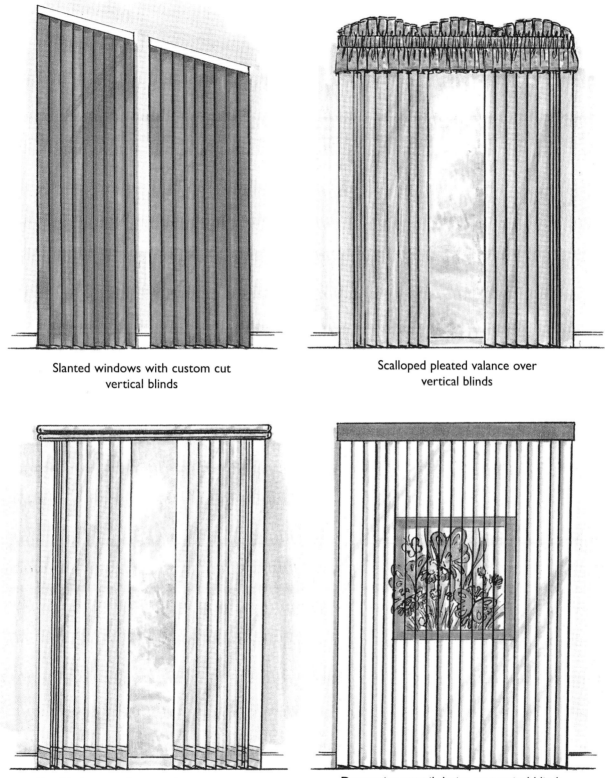

Slanted windows with custom cut
vertical blinds

Scalloped pleated valance over
vertical blinds

Double brass rods over vertical blinds with
brass trim at bottom

Decorative stencil design on vertical blinds

CHALLENGING WINDOWS

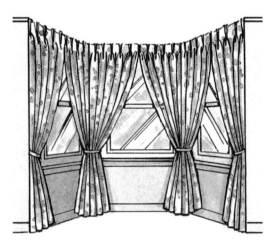

HAVE YOU EVER LOOKED AT YOUR WINDOWS WITH DISMAY, wondering how to treat them without it ending in complete disaster? First, study the many different types of window shapes in homes today and then discover how one challenging window can be treated successfully in a variety of ways.

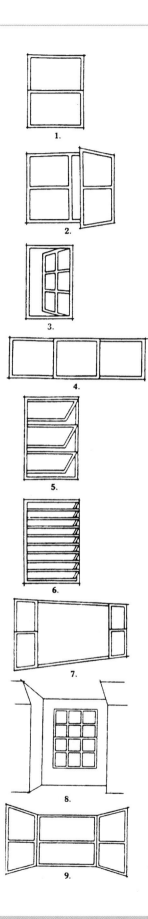

1. Double hung
The most common of all window types, it has two sashes, one or both of which slide up and down. Unless it is too long and narrow or in the wrong location, this window is usually one of the easiest to decorate.

2. In-swinging casement
Opens into the room. If it is not decorated properly, curtains and draperies may tangle with the window as it is opened or closed.

3. Out-swinging casement
Opens outward. Both in-swinging and out-swinging casements may be operated by a crank, or simply moved by hand. Easily decorated.

4. Ranch (strip)
Most often a wide window set high off the floor. Usually has sliding sashes and is common to most ranch type houses. It requires special consideration when decorating to make it attractive.

5. Awning
Has wide, horizontal sashes that open outward to any angle; can usually be left open when it's raining. Unless it is awkwardly placed or shaped, it's easy to decorate.

6. Jalousie
Identified by narrow, horizontal strips of glass that open by means of a crank to any desired angle. Decorating problems result only when the shape or location is unusual.

7. Picture
One designed to frame an outside view. It may consist of one large, fixed pane of glass, in which case the window cannot be opened. Or, it may have moveable sections on one or both sides of a fixed pane (or above and below) which can be opened for ventilation. Sometimes there are decorating problems, but in general, a picture window is a big opportunity for creativity.

8. Dormer
Usually a small window projecting from the house in an alcove-like extension of the room. It requires its own treatment.

9. Bay
Three or more window set at an angle to each other in a recessed area. Plenty of imagination can be used.

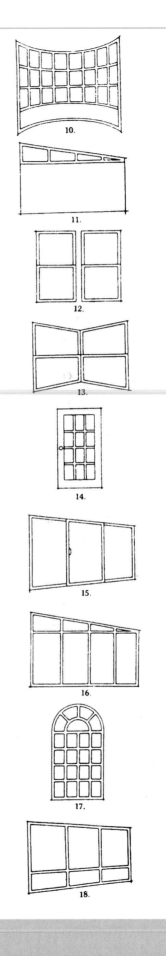

10. Bow
A curved window, sometimes called a circular bay.

11. Slant
Often called a "cathedral" window, it usually encompasses an entire wall. Its main characteristic is the angle at the top where the window follows the line of a slanting roof. This top slanting line often causes decorating concern, but the problem can be solved very effectively.

12. Double
Side by side windows. If there are more than one, they are often called multiple windows. Most often treated as a single unit, always think of them as one decorating element.

13. Corner
Two windows that meet at the corner of a room.

14. French doors
Sometimes called French windows. They come in pairs and often open onto a porch or patio. Usually, they need special decorating to look their best. Additionally, the treatment must not impede egress.

15. Sliding glass doors
Today's functional version of French doors. They are often set into a regular wall, but are sometimes part of a modern "glass wall." Either way, they need special decor that allows them to serve as doors yet provide nighttime privacy.

16. Clerestory
A shallow window set near the ceiling. Usually should be decorated inconspicuously. In modern architecture, it is sometimes placed in the scope of a beamed ceiling, in which case it should rarely be decorated at all.

17. Palladian
An arched top window with straight panes below the arch.

18. Glass wall
Usually a group of basic window units made to fit together, forming a veritable "wall" of windows. Curtains and draperies often require special planning.

Door with window and skylights

Solution 1

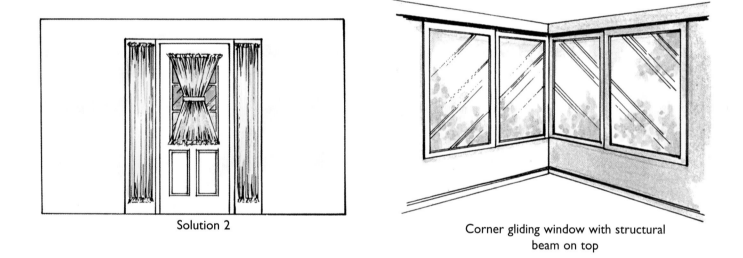

Solution 2

Corner gliding window with structural
beam on top

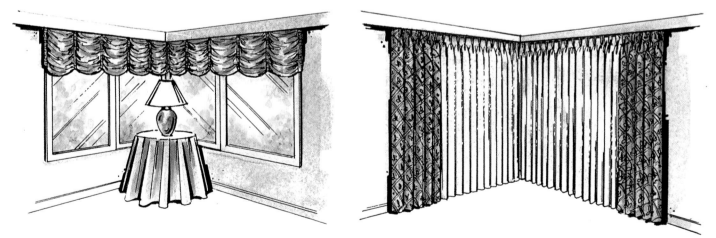

Solution 1

Solution 2

Corner windows

Solution 1

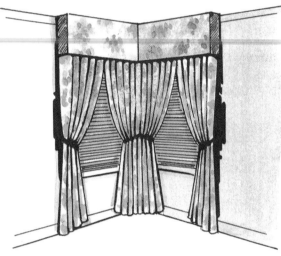

Solution 2

Solution 3

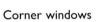

Solution 4

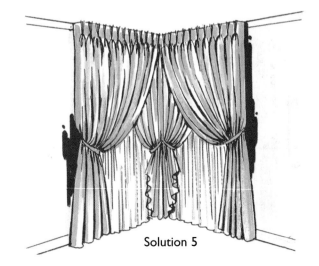

Solution 5

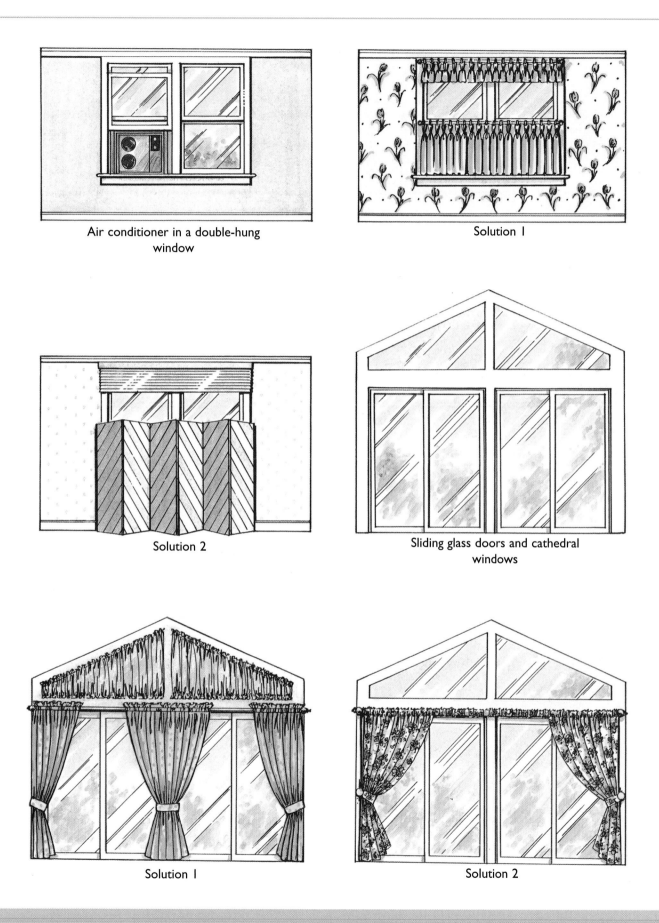

Air conditioner in a double-hung
window

Solution 1

Solution 2

Sliding glass doors and cathedral
windows

Solution 1

Solution 2

Solution 3

Solution 4

Solution 5

Solution 6

Clerestory windows

Solution 1

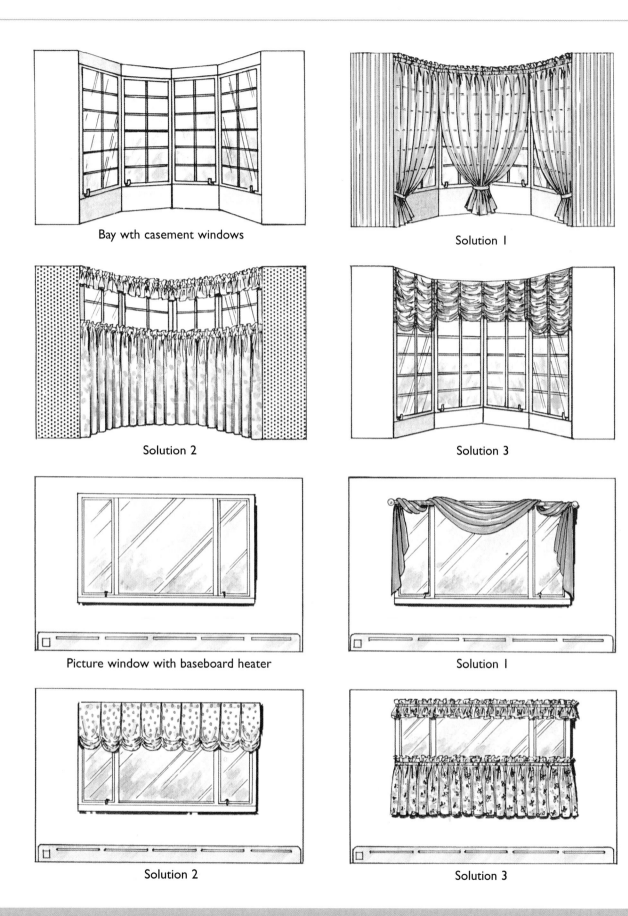

Bay wth casement windows

Solution 1

Solution 2

Solution 3

Picture window with baseboard heater

Solution 1

Solution 2

Solution 3

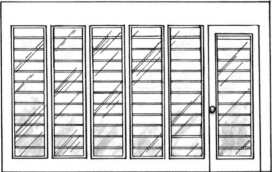

Jalousie windows and doors

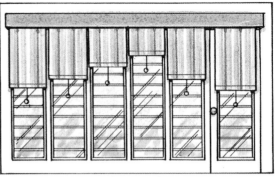

Solution 1

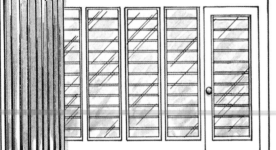

Solution 2

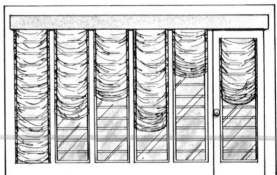

Solution 3

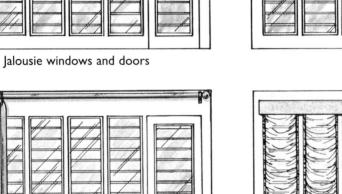

French doors

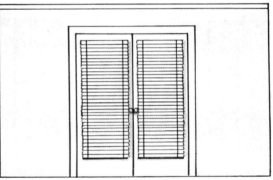

Solution 1

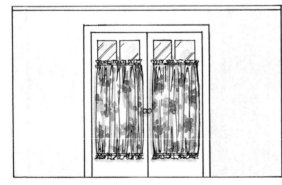

Solution 2

Solution 3

Triple double-hung windows

Solution 1

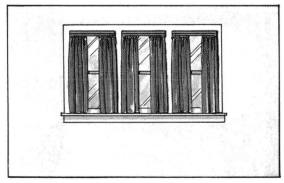

Solution 2

Solution 3

Bay with double hung windows

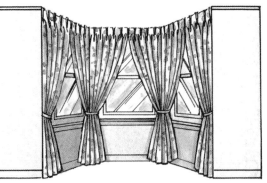

Solution 1

Solution 2

Solution 3

Arched top windows

Solution 1

Solution 2

Solution 3

Solution 4

Solution 5

IN COLOR, IMAGES HAVE A WAY OF IMPRESSING THEMSELVES upon us, dazzling or dismaying us with their patterns and tones. In black and white, the onus is upon us to imagine our favorite shades. Over the next pages, feel free to photocopy and get out your coloring pencils and pens. Let your imagination take flight and soon you will uncover the window treatment or room accessory of your dreams.

50 | 51
52 | 53

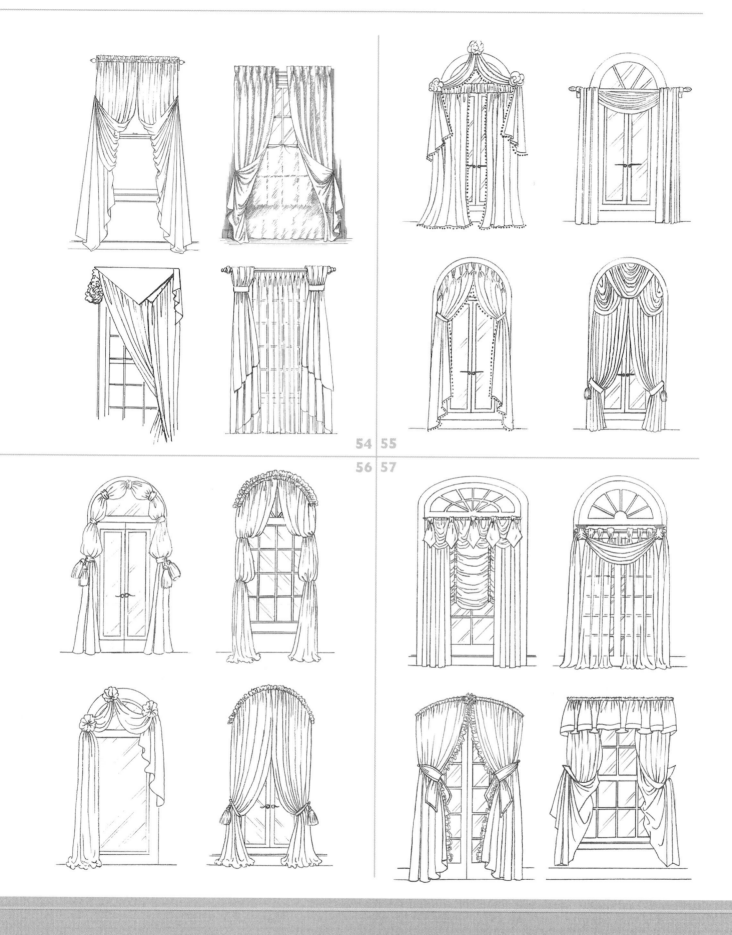

54 | 55

56 | 57

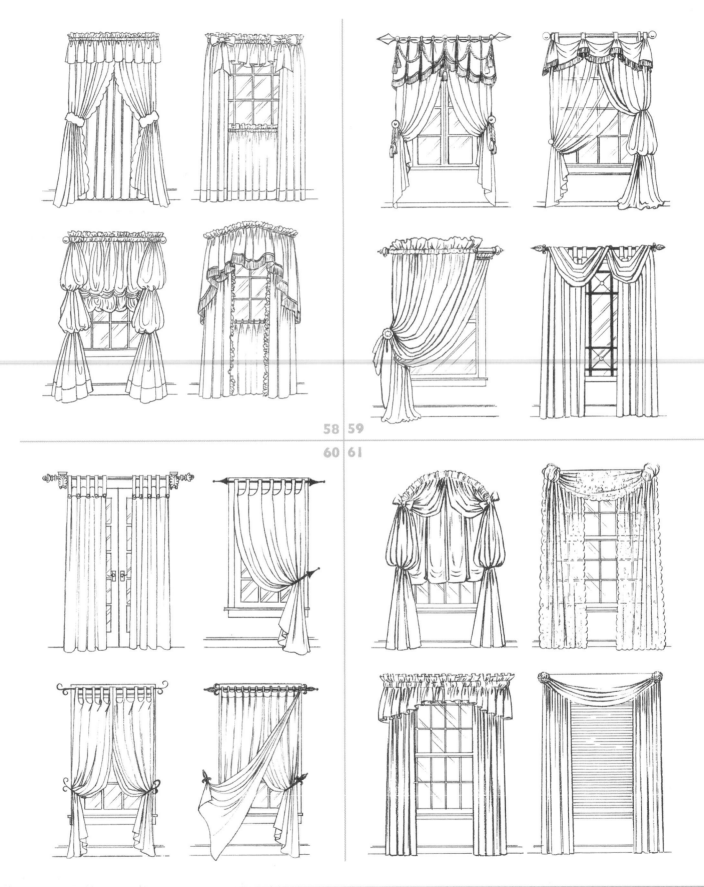

58 | 59
60 | 61

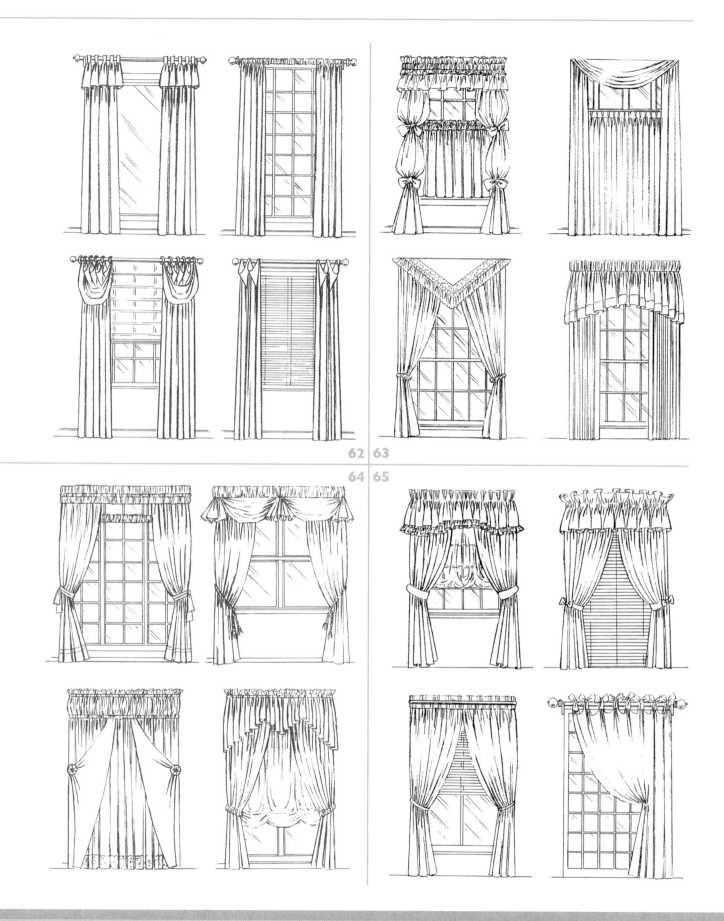

62 | 63
64 | 65

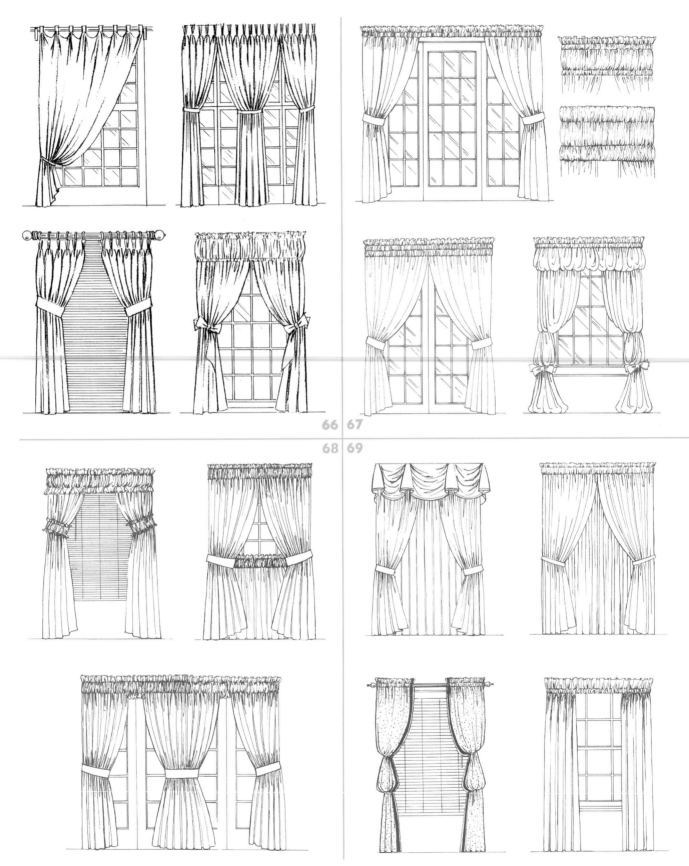

66 | 67

68 | 69

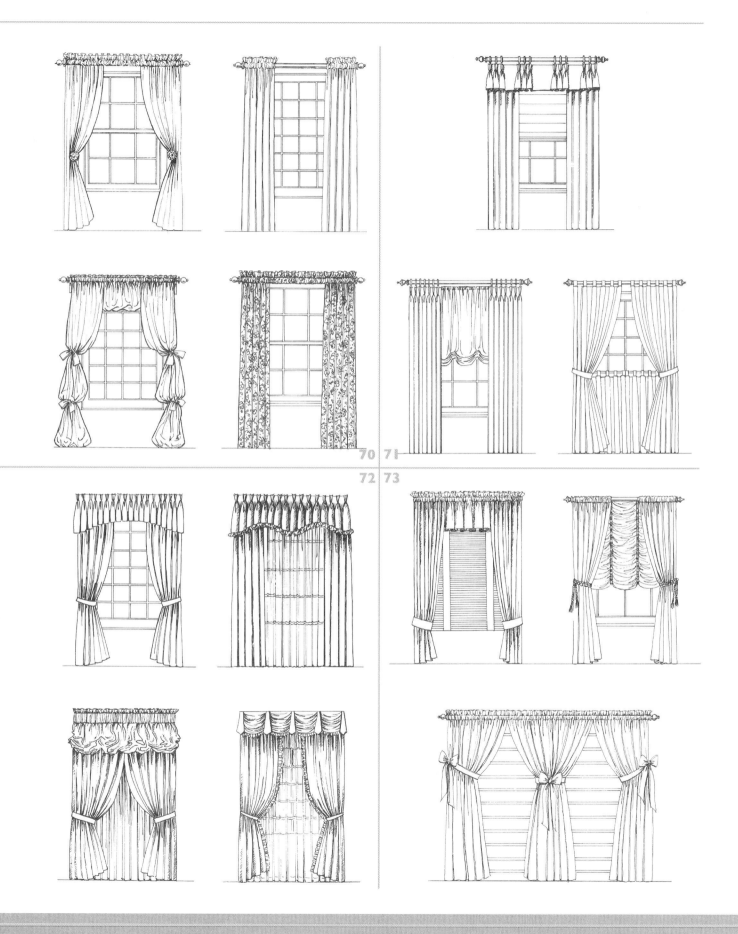

70 71

72 73

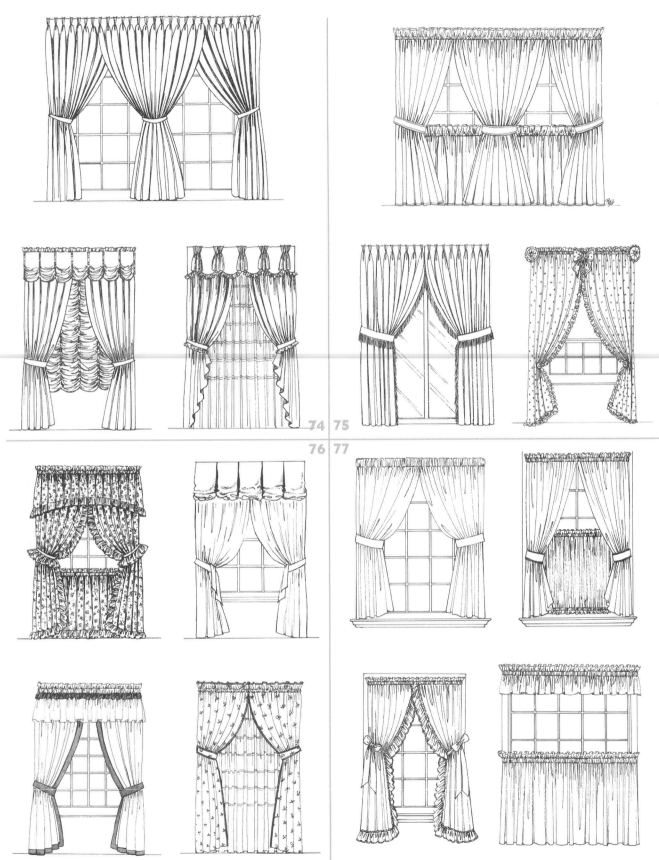

74 75
76 77

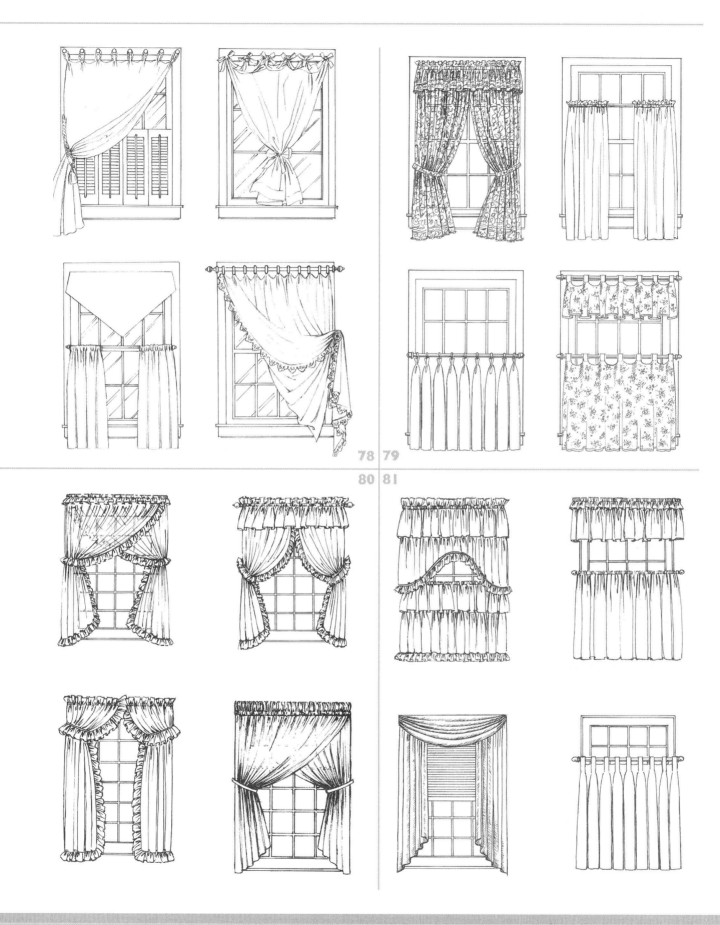

78 79
80 81

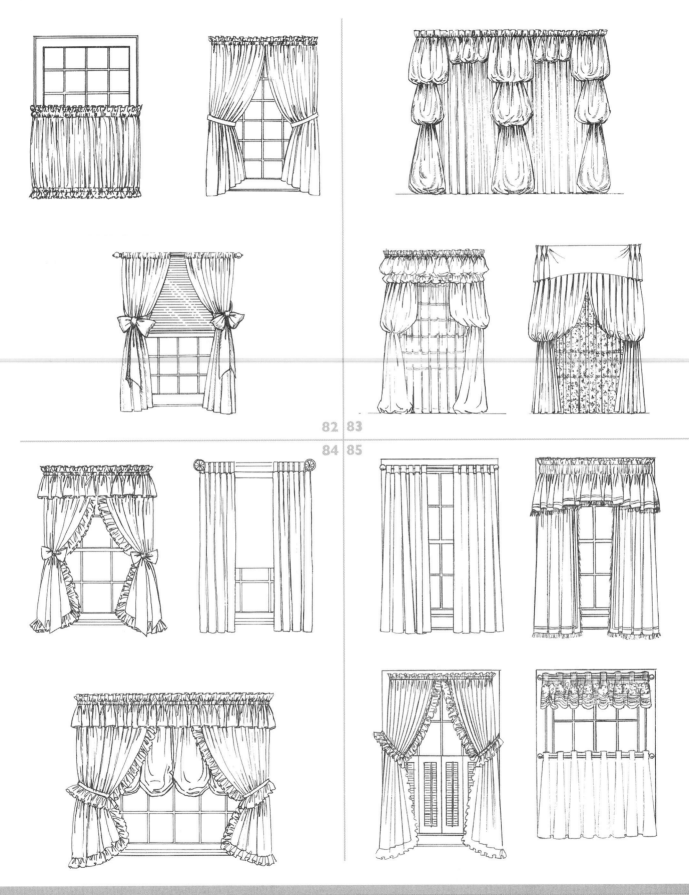

82 | 83
84 | 85

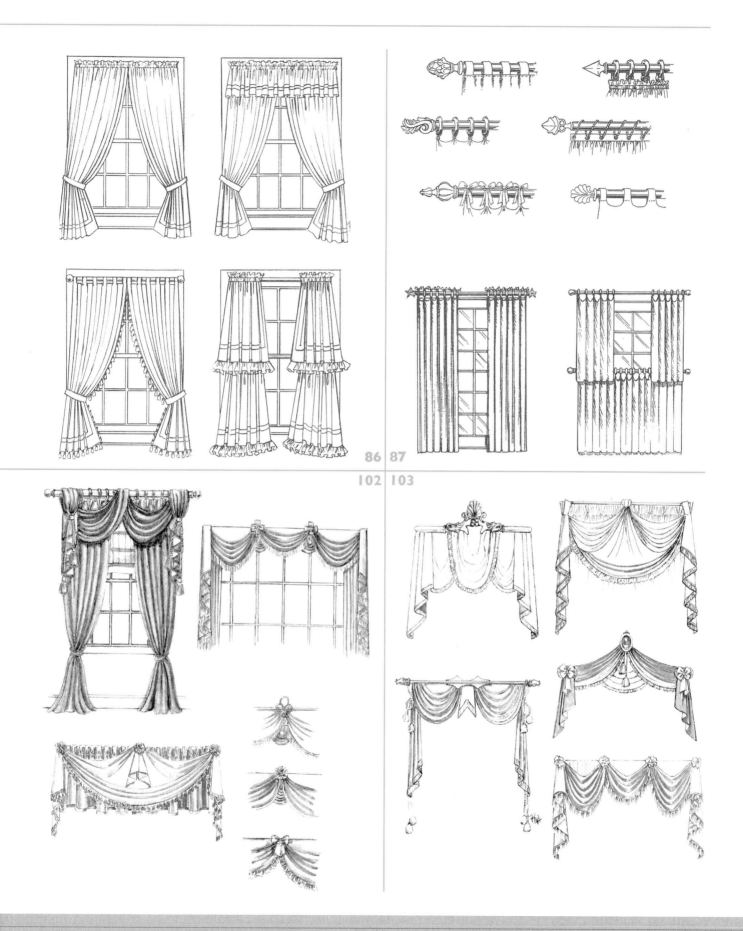

86 | 87
102 | 103

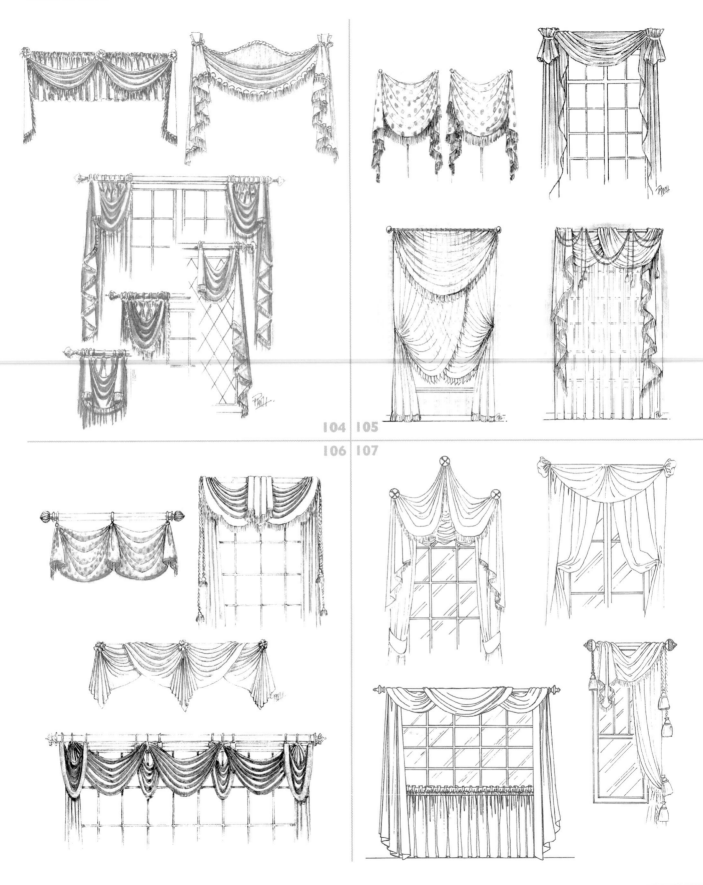

104 | 105
106 | 107

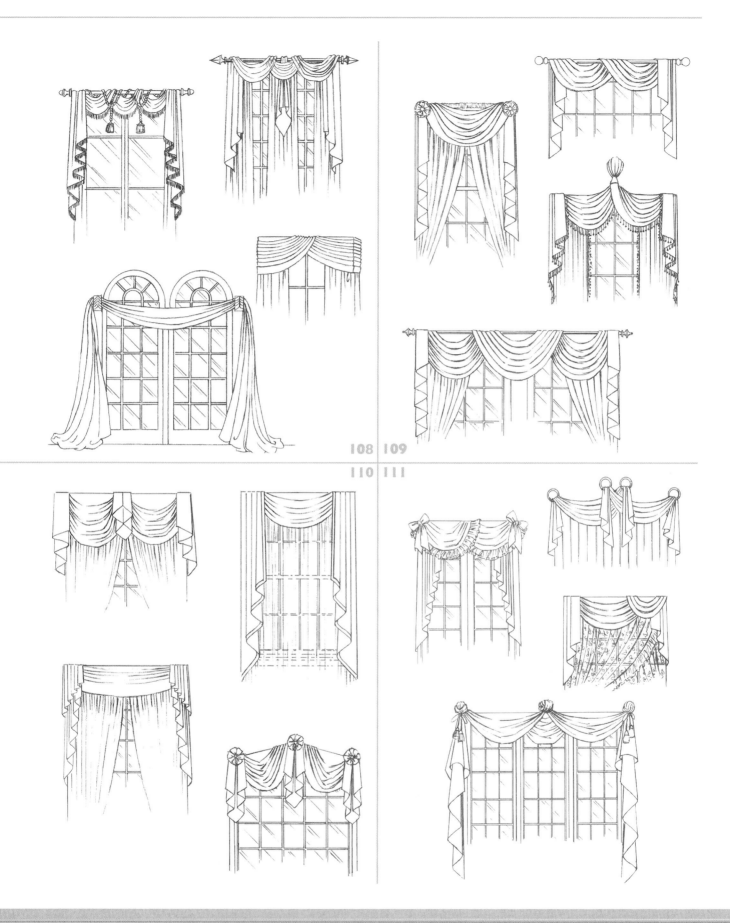

108 | 109
110 | 111

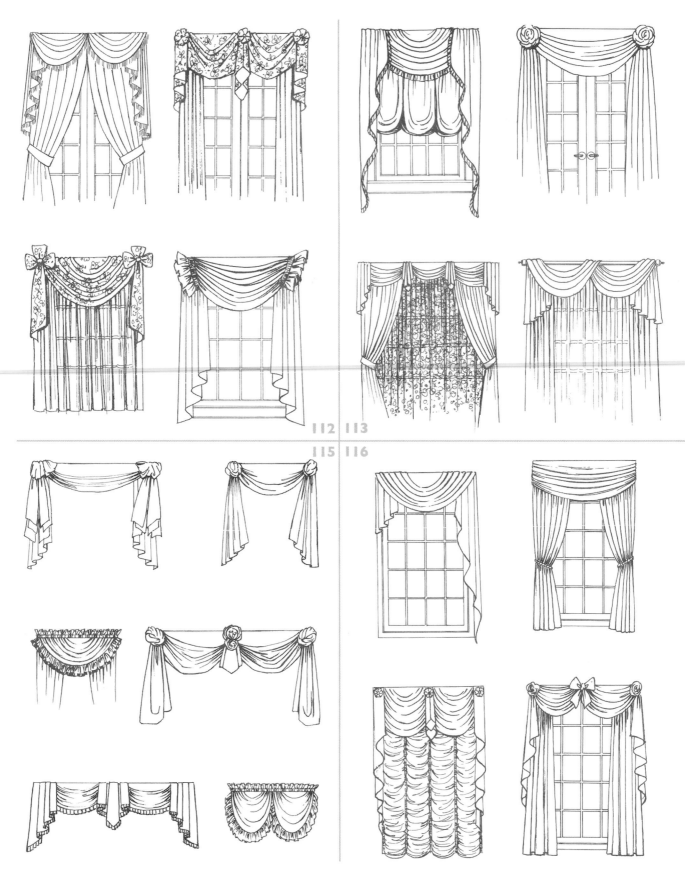

112 113
115 116

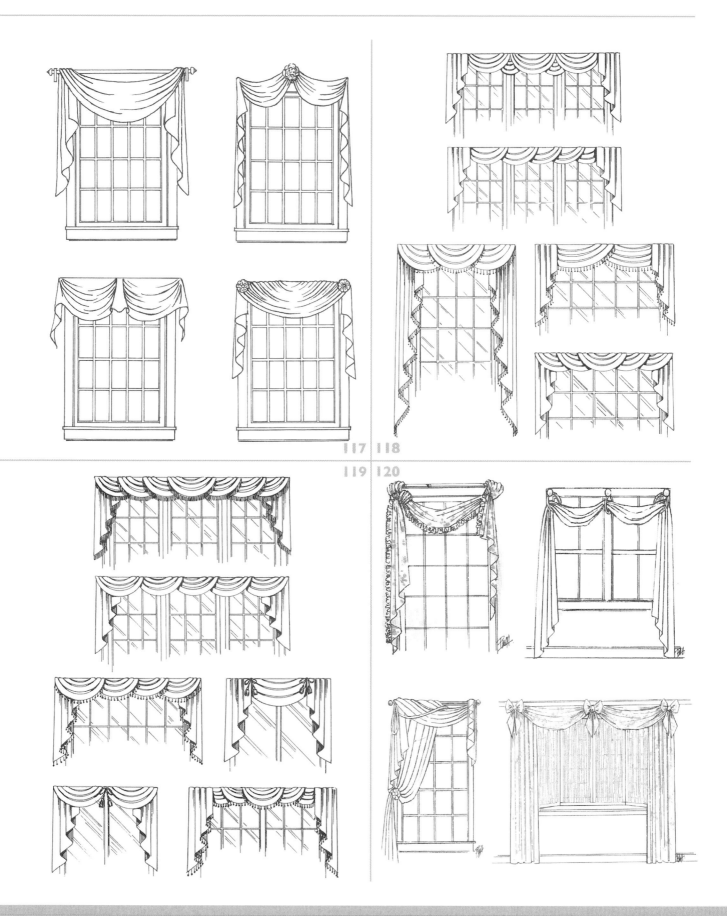

117 | 118

119 | 120

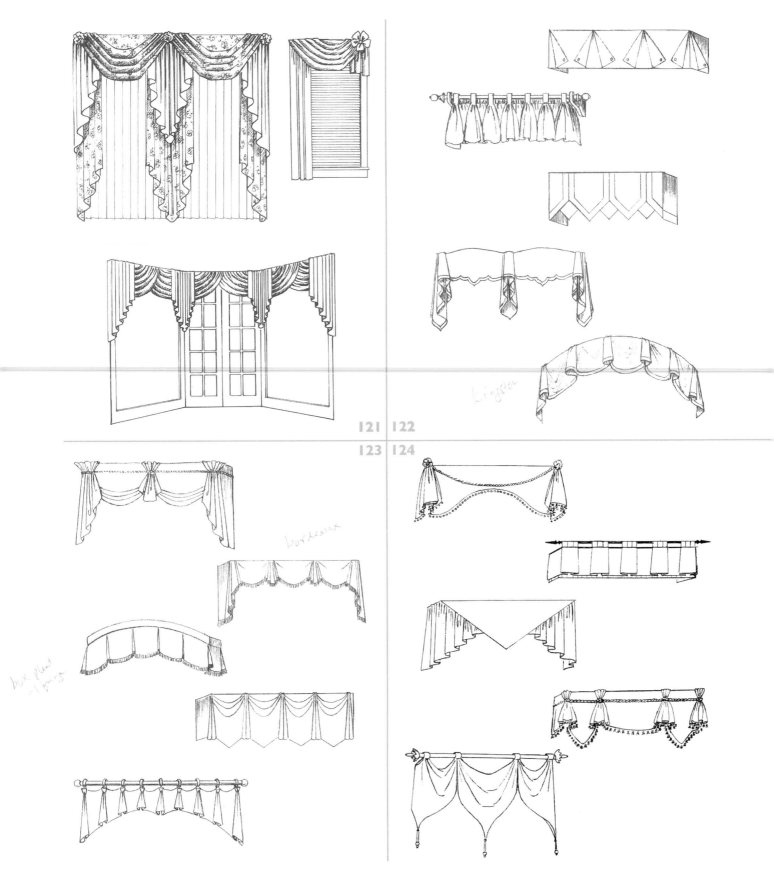

121 | 122

123 | 124

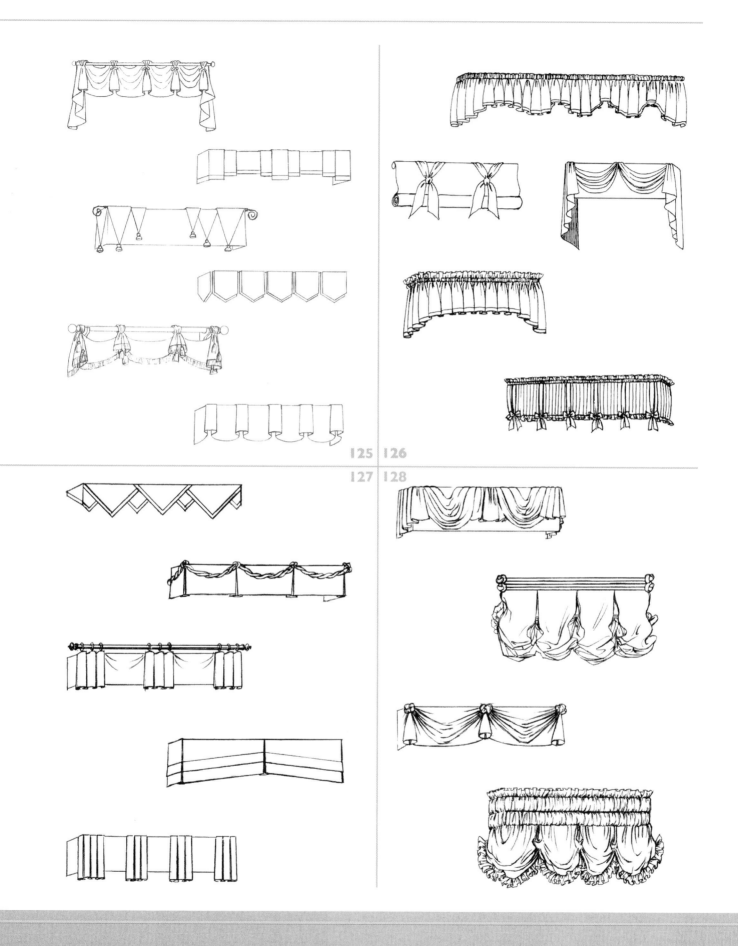

125 | 126
127 | 128

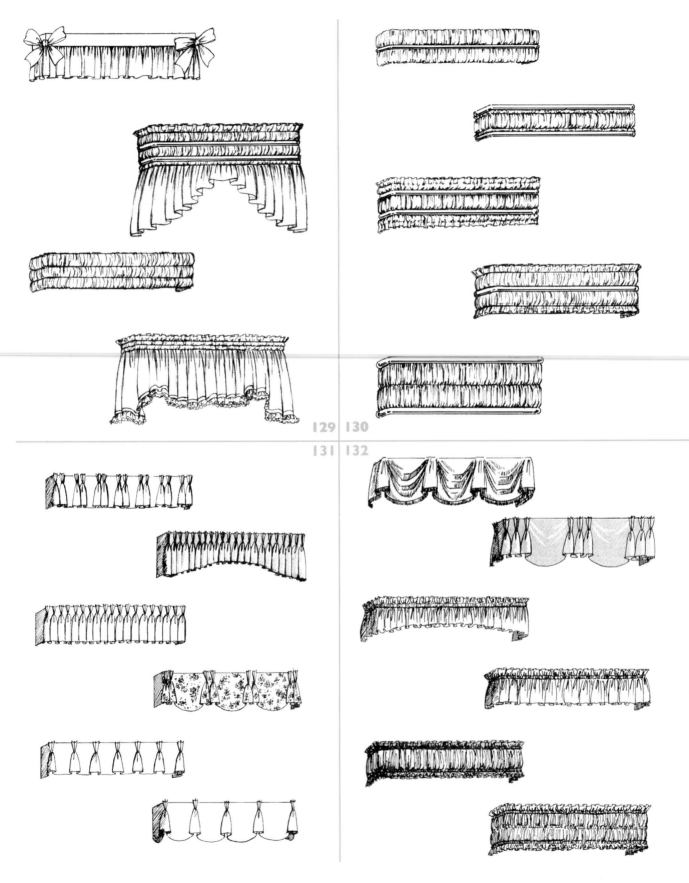

129 | 130
131 | 132

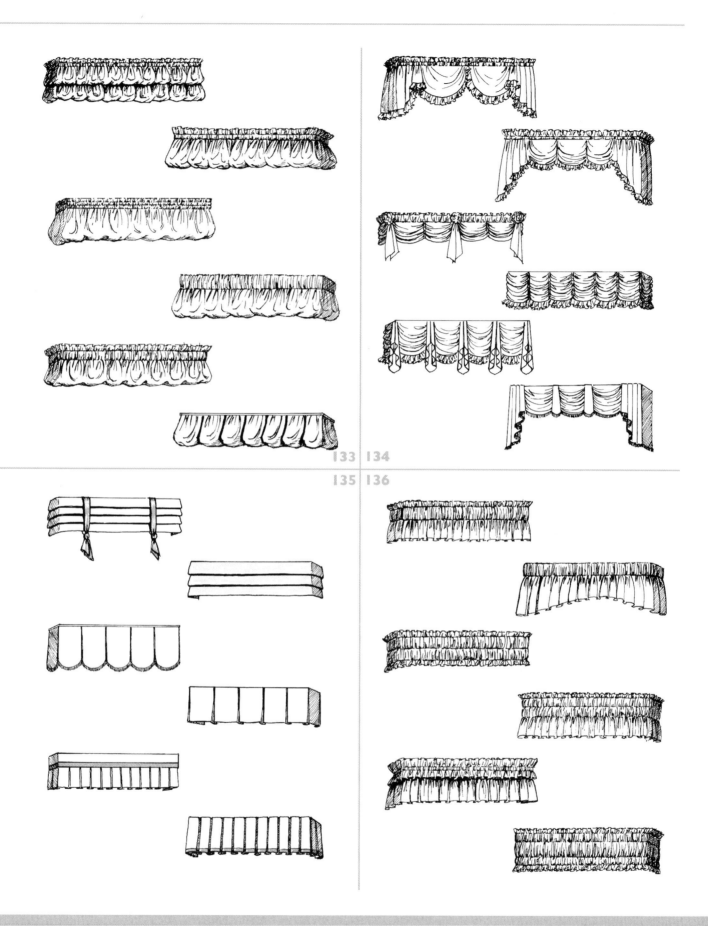

133 | 134
135 | 136

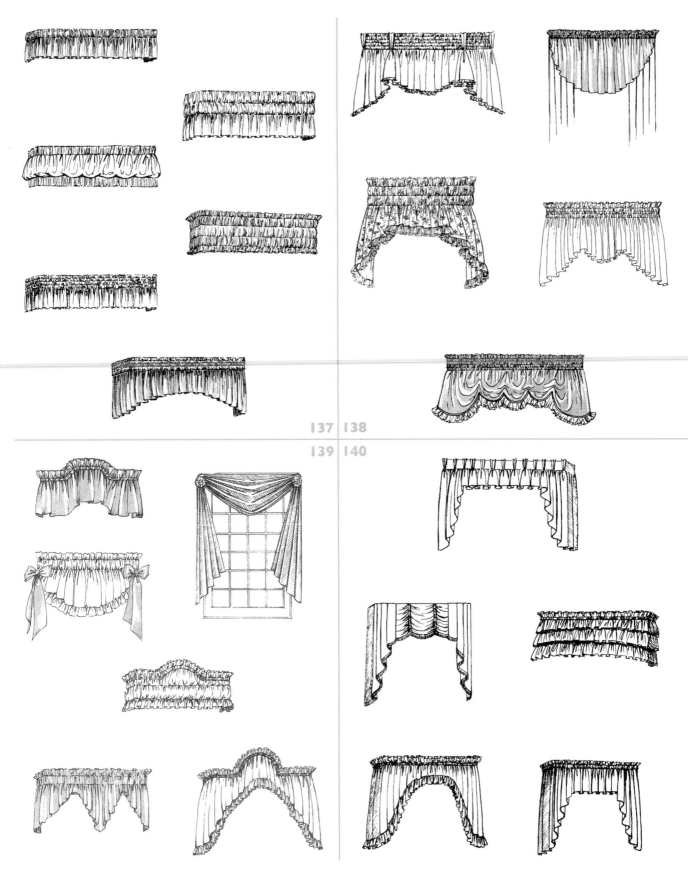

137 | 138

139 | 140

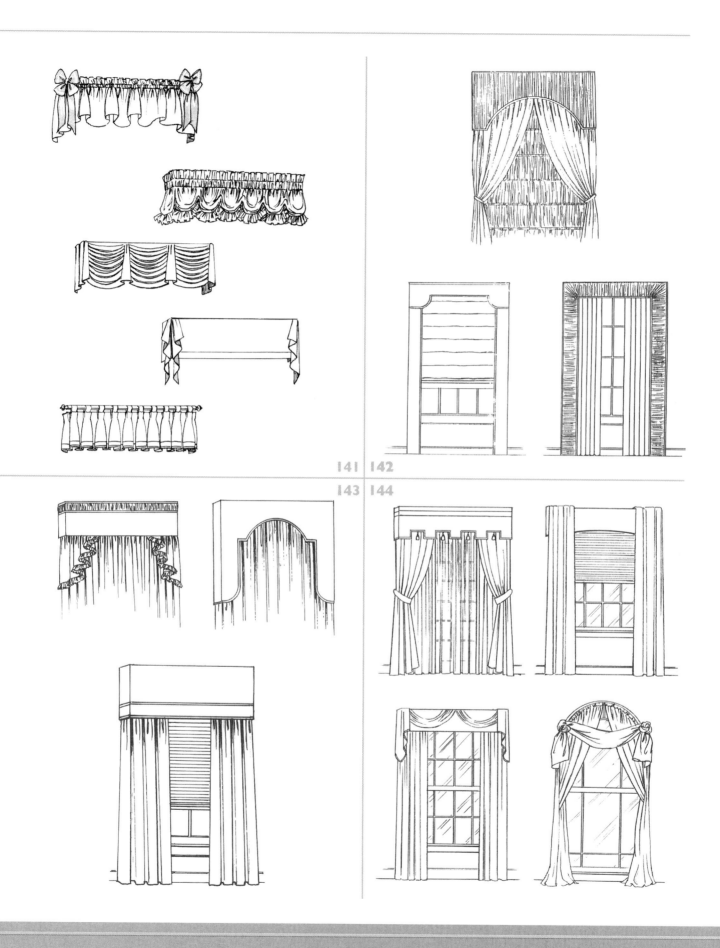

141 142

143 144

145 | 146
147 | 148

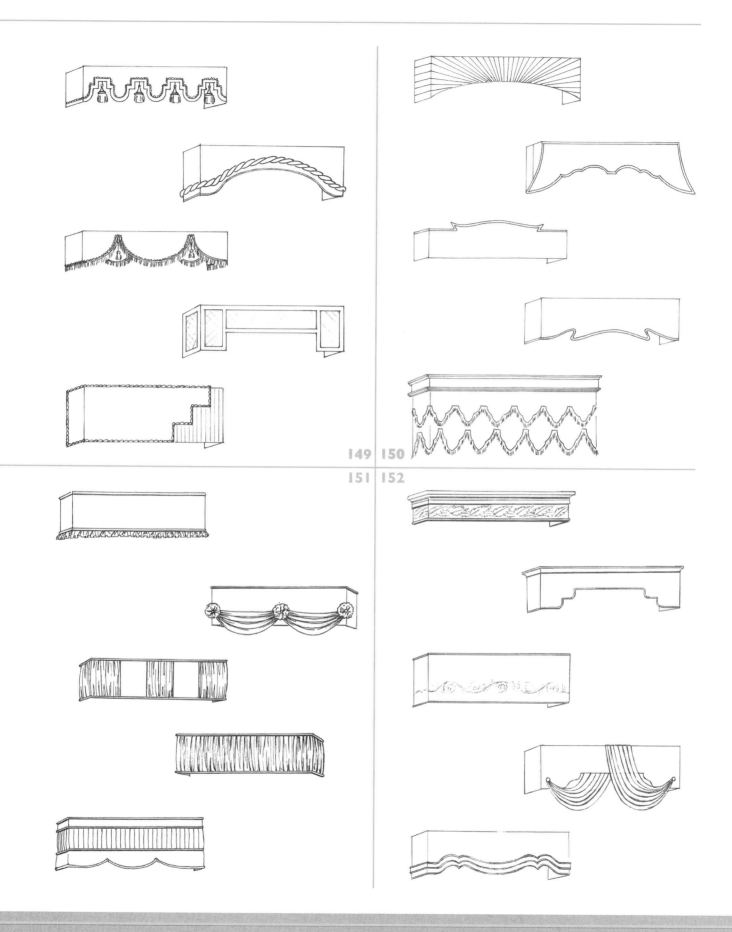

149 150
151 152

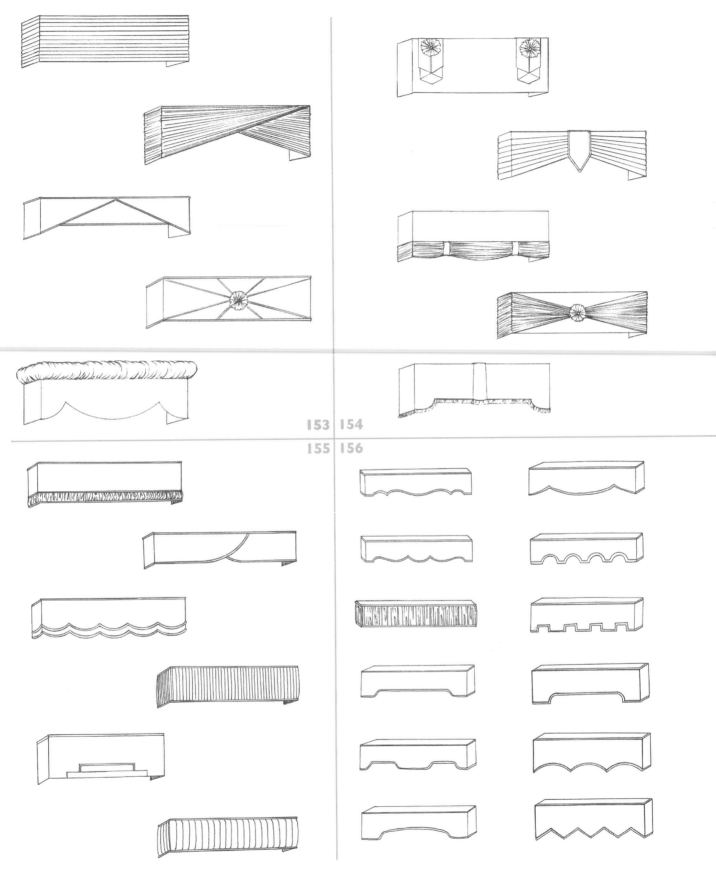

153 | 154
155 | 156

157 | 158
174 | 175

176 177
178 179

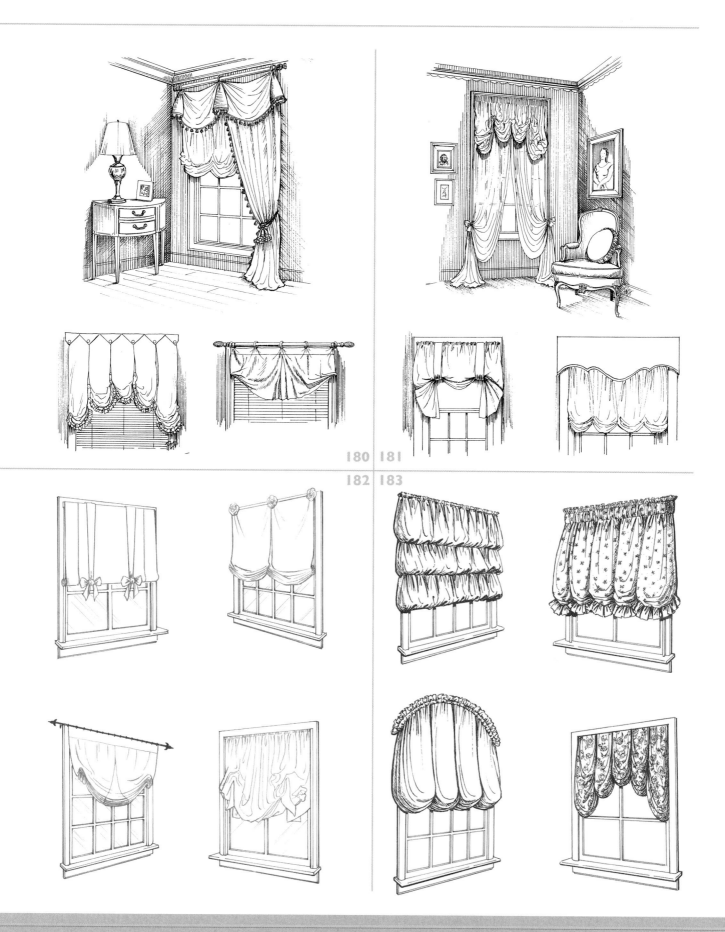

180 | 181
182 | 183

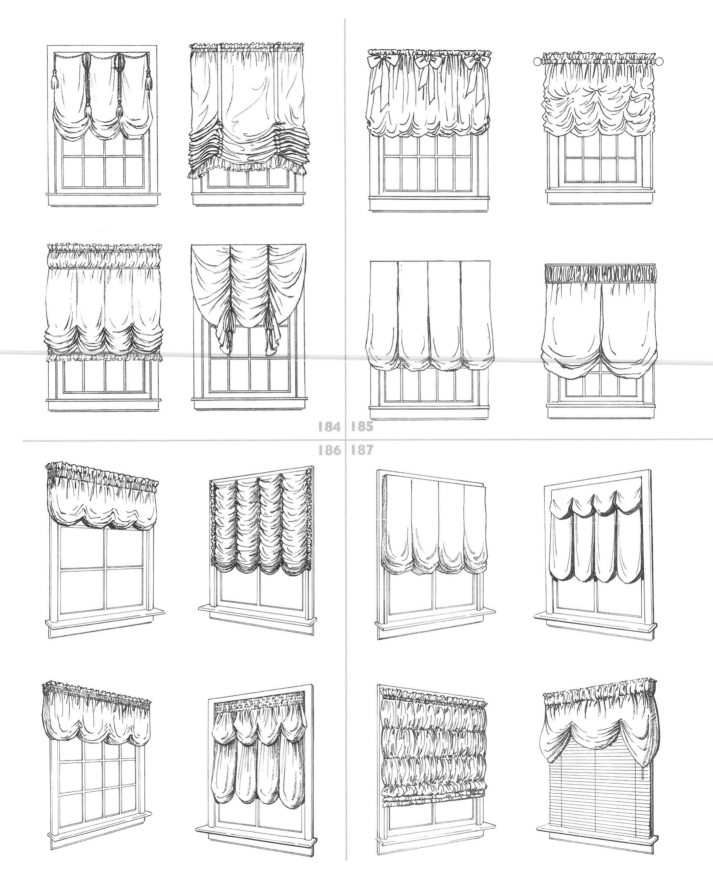

184 | 185

186 | 187

188 | 189

190 | 200

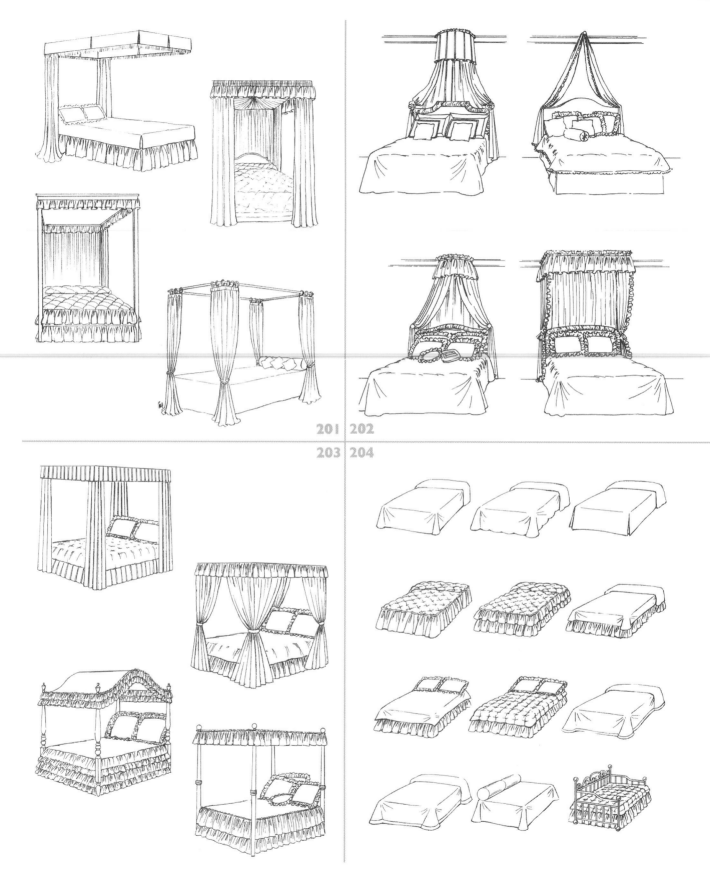

201 | 202
203 | 204

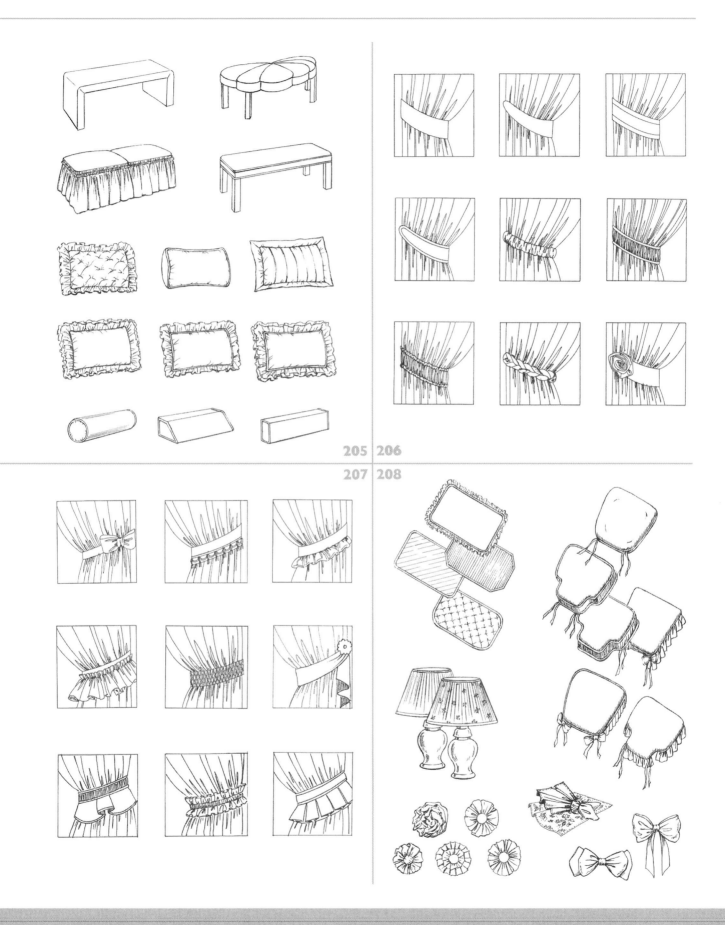

205 | 206
207 | 208

209 | 210

211 | 212

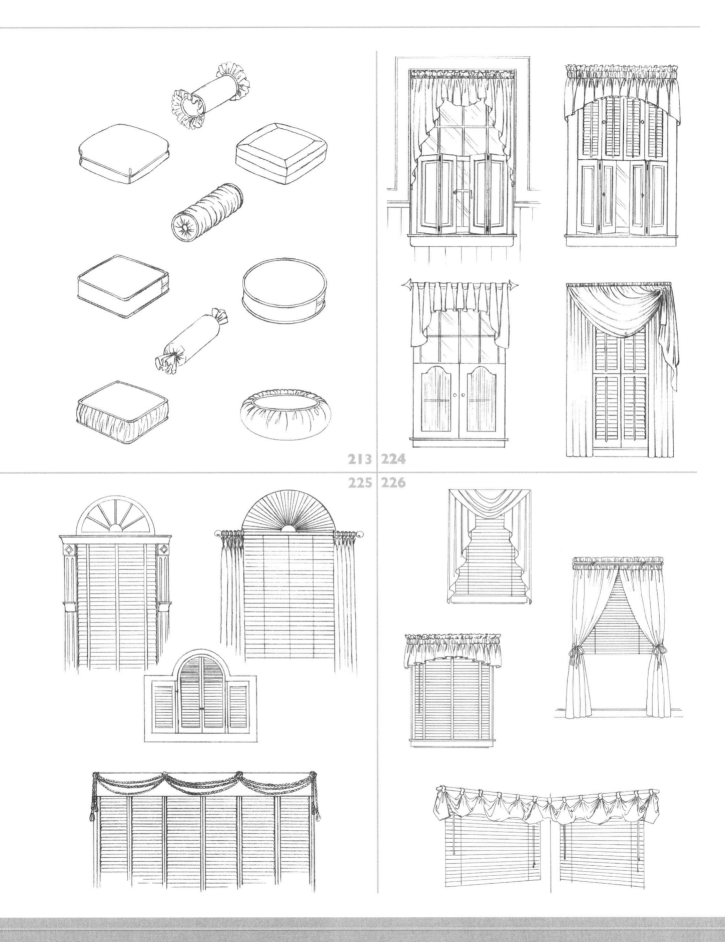

213 | 224
225 | 226

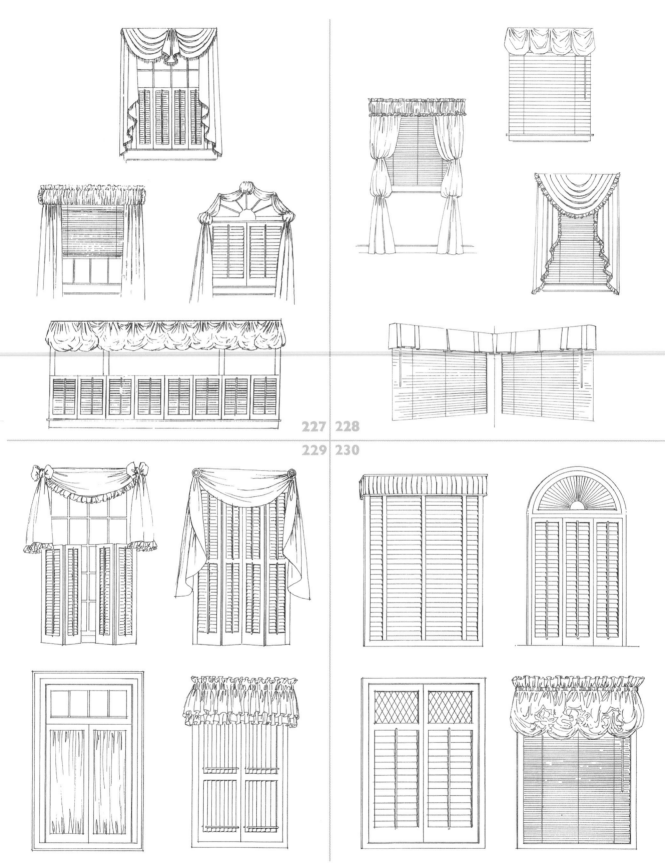

227 228
229 230

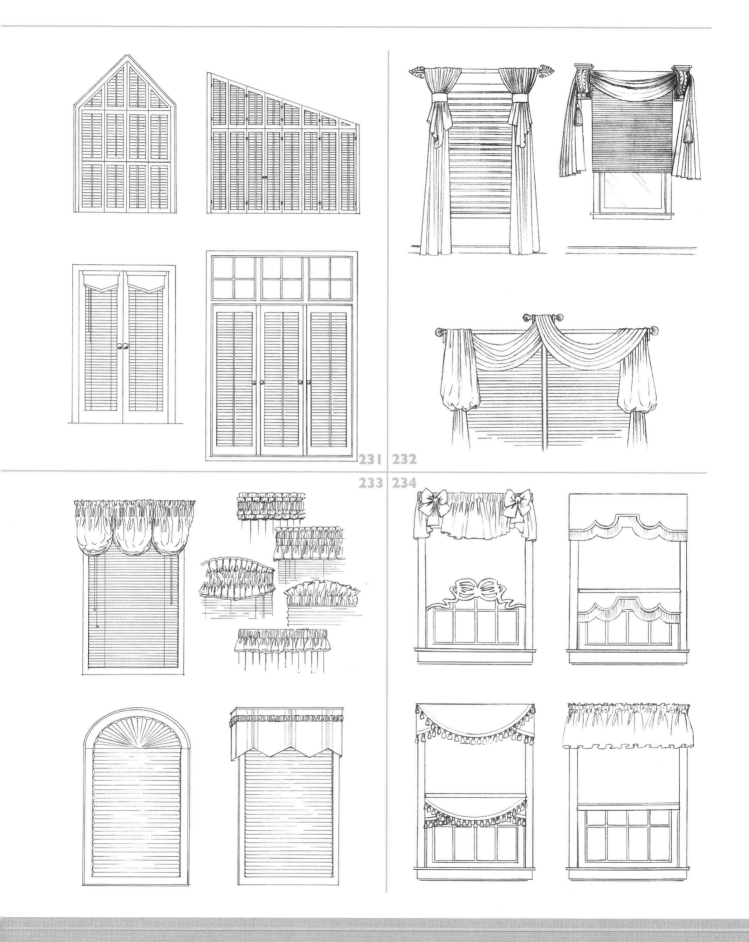

231 | 232
233 | 234

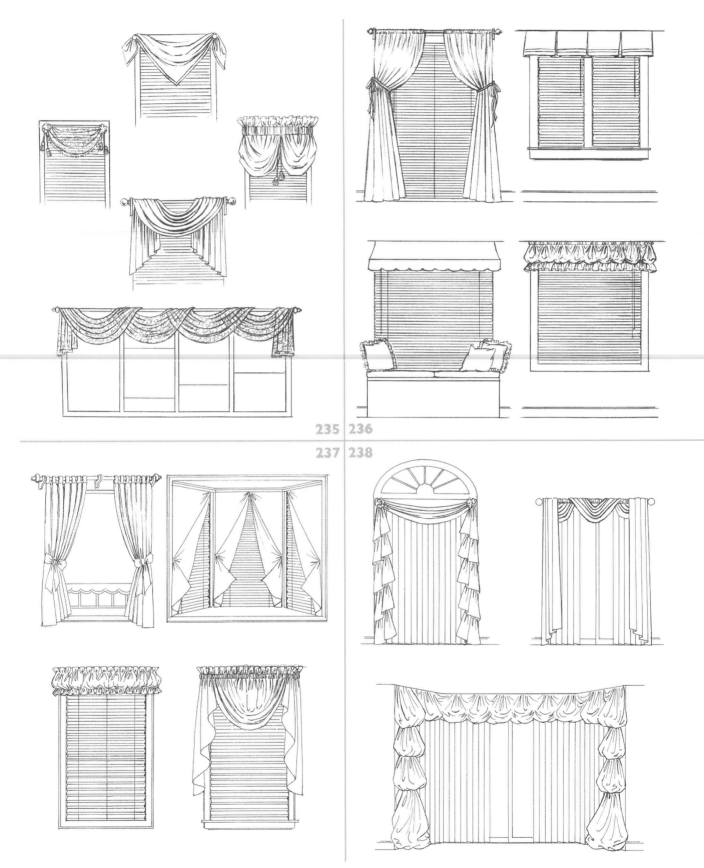

235 | 236
237 | 238

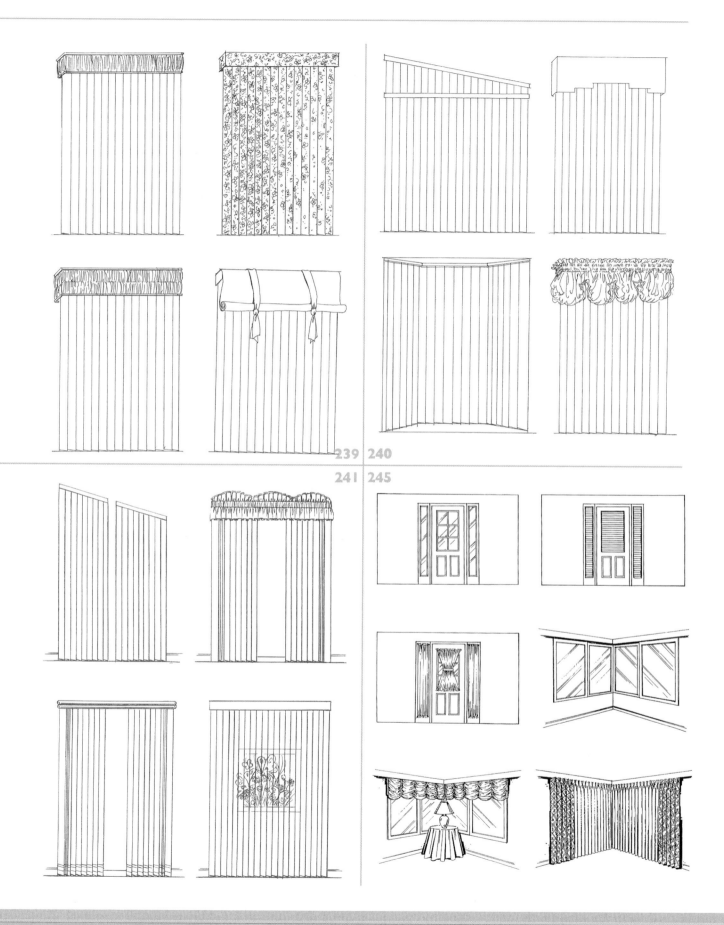

239 | 240
241 | 245

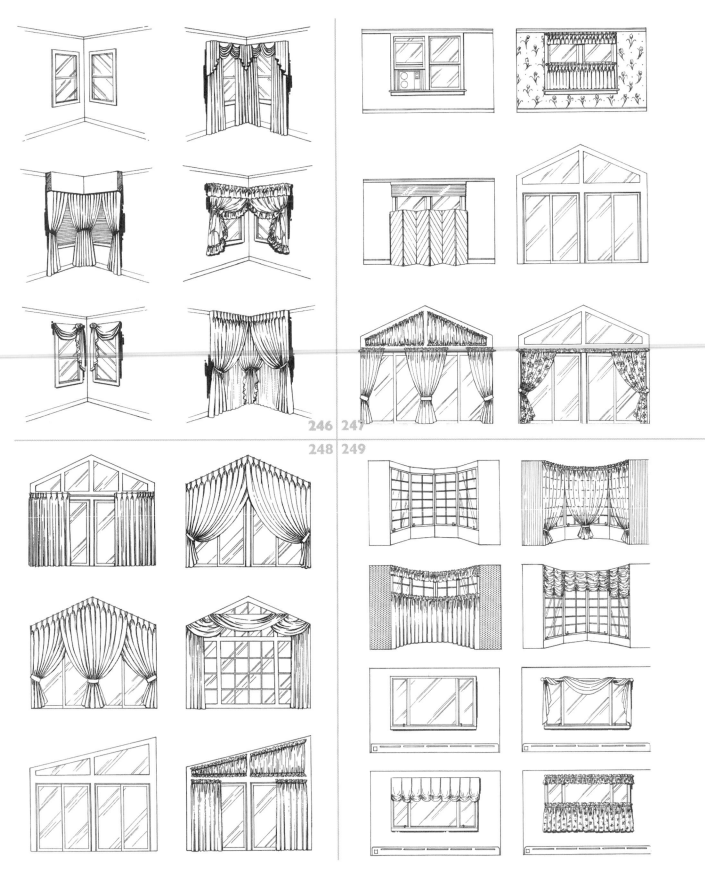

246 | 247

248 | 249

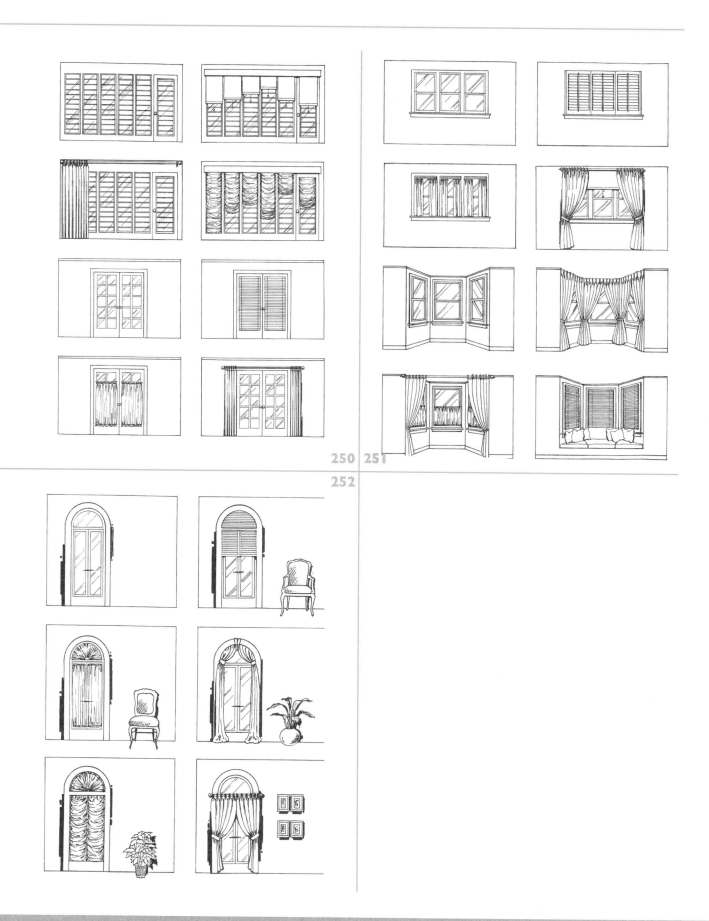

250 251

252

GLOSSARY OF DECORATING TERMS

A

A-frame window: Very contemporary house structures sometimes form an "A" shape. When draperies are used, they hang from the cross-beam of the "A," or they can be fabricated and installed to conform to the shape of the window.

A La Duchesse: A type of bed supported with a canopy suspension from the ceiling rather than posts. It is also known as an angel bed.

Accordion pleat: Single large pleats which are often used as a method of fan folding in pleated draperies before installing, or can be used in contract draperies by snapping onto channel slides.

Allowance: A customary variation from an "exact" measurement, taken for the purpose of anticipated needs.

Appliqué: The application of a second, decorated layer of fabric onto a base piece of cloth.

Apron: A piece of wood trim beneath the windowsill.

Architectural rodding: Used for contract draperies, a sturdy, sleek or traverse channel.

Architrave: The molding around an arch or wooden surrounding to a window or door frame.

Art glass: Glass which is cut at an angle (other than a right angle), stained and etched, and used for hard window treatments.

Art Nouveau: An historical design movement of the Victorian Era, dating from 1890 to 1910. The motifs are based on flowing plant forms.

Asymmetrical balance: A type of design in which the entire arrangement has a balance, but each side of a central point is different.

Austrian shade: A shade having ruche down the whole side length, creating billows when the shade is raised.

Automated exterior rolling shutters: A treatment used for insulation and privacy purposes, in which the exterior of a window has metal panels, which roll down mechanically over the glass.

Awning window: A type of window that can swing out due to a hinged top.

B

Backstitch: A reverse-stitch used to keep the stitches from coming undone at the ends. Several stitches are sewn at the beginning and end of any seam.

Balloon shade: Shades with vertical rows of horizontally gathered fabric, which can be drawn up to form strips of pleated or gathered trim.

Balloon tiebacks: Curtains which, when tied back, form a rounded sort of cloud shape.

Bamboo shade: A natural light-softening shade, drawn by hand using a cord and made of woven panels of split bamboo. Also called a Bali blind.

Baroque: An elaborate interior design period dating from 1643 to 1730 in France and 1660 to 1714 in England.

Bar tack: A sewing machine operation of repeated stitches concentrated to secure the lowest portion of drapery pleats.

Basement windows: Opposite of awning windows, these windows swing inward due to a hinged bottom.

Basting: A technique used in sewing to temporarily fasten layers of fabric using long, loose stitches.

Baton: A rod or wand used to hand draw traverse draperies.

Bay window: A large projecting type of window made of a group of windows set at angles to each other and joined to each other on some sides.

Bell valance: A gathered or pleated valance that has a number of bell-like shapes at bottom hemline.

Bias binding: A strip of fabric used for added strength when binding edges of fabric and closing piping. The fabric is cut in a slanted manner from selvage to selvage.

Bishop's sleeve curtains: Tie-back curtains which have been bloused at least two times.

Blind: A hard treatment for a window, consisting of a series of horizontal panels.

Bottom hem: The turned part forming a finished edge at bottom of a drapery.

Bow window: A large projecting type of window that is curved or semi-circular.

Box pleat: A fold of cloth sewn into place to create fullness in a drapery. Box pleats are evenly spaced and stitched.

Bracket: Metal piece attached to the wall or casing to sup-port a drapery or curtain rod.

Braid: A woven ribbon that may be used for trimming or can be added to edges of draperies and accessories.

Bull's-eye window: A circular window glazed with flat or arched glass.

Butterfly pleat: A two-part pleat that flares out at the top and is bar-tacked at the bottom.

C

Café curtain: A traversing or non-traversing drapery, designed as a tier. The heading can be various styles. They can be set at a variety of heights to control ventilation, view and light.

Café rod: A small, round decorative rod that comes in white, brass or woodgrain finish, used to mount café curtains that do not have a rod pocket. Café rods are meant to be seen and add an additional decorative touch to the curtain treatment.

Canopy: A fabric window topper created by sewing pockets into fabric panels and inserting a rod with a small projection at the top of the panel, a rod with a larger projection at the bottom.

Cantonniere: A three-sided shaped or straight cornice that frames a window across the top and down the two sides. Made of a hardboard, padded and covered with fabric.

Cape Cod curtain: A café curtain decorated by a ruffle around the bottom and sides. This is also called a ruffle-round curtain.

Carriers: Small runners installed in a traverse rod which hold a drapery pin or hook.

Cartridge pleat: A fold of cloth sewn into place to create fullness in a drapery. This is a round pleat 2 to 2½ inches in depth. Roundness is created by stuffing crinoline or paper (removed for cleaning).

Cascade: A fall of fabric that descends in a zigzag line from a drapery heading or top treatment.

Cased heading: A curtain heading with a simple, hemmed top, in which a rod is inserted.

Casement: (1) A cloth drapery that is of an open-weave material but more opaque than a sheer. (2) A type of vertically hinged window, whose panes open by sliding sideways or cranking outward.

Casing (window): Wooden frame around a window.

Catchstitch: A stitch used for hemming raw edges, and then covered by a piece of fabric.

Cathedral window: A window which points upward, and is formed at an angle.

Center draw: One pair of draperies that draw open and close exactly at a window's center point.

Center support: A metal grip which is used to support a traverse rod from above and prevents rod form sagging in the middle, but does not interfere with rod operation.

Clerestory windows: A series of small windows that let in light and air. These are placed high on the wall to allow complete privacy.

Colonial: A design period common prior to the revolutionary war in America. It is typically dated from 1608 to 1790.

Corbel bay: A second story bay window.

Cord: A cable yarn that can be made from either cotton or synthetic materials. It is used for various reasons including holding blinds and shades together, and as a means for drawing traverse draperies, shades and blinds.

Corner window: A window that wraps a corner of the building at right angles.

Cornice: A shallow, box-like structure, usually made of wood, fastened across the top of a window to conceal the drapery hardware.

Cornice board: A horizontal board used as support for a cornice or as foundation for swags and tails.

Cornice pole: A curtain pole having rings and used for heavy curtains.

Corona drape: A drapery that is hung at the top of a bed from a semi-circular bracket or a pole.

Cottage curtains: A term used to describe curtains displayed in a casual or informal manner.

Country curtains: A casual curtain treatment with ruffles at valance, bottom, sides and ties. The curtain is shirred a maximum of five times in fullness and is usually made with plain or tiny-printed fabric.

Coverage: A term used to describe the fullness of fabric used on a window.

Crown glass: A particular type of glass consisting of hand-blown crowns, measuring about one meter in diameter.

Curtain: A window covering either hung from rings, or made with a casing so that it slips over a rod. Curtains are informal window coverings.

Custom glazing: Unusual sized or oddly shaped window glass, which is custom made and installed.

Custom-made draperies: Draperies made to order in a workroom or decorator shop.

Cut length: The length after allowances have been made for heading and hem.

Cut width: The width that the fabric should be cut after allowances have been made.

D

Decorator rods: Hardware used for the purpose of decorating, that is meant to be seen in the open. Usually made from chrome, wood, brass or antique wrought iron.

Diaphanous sheers: Drapery used for the purpose of daytime privacy. The finely woven transparent fabrics filter out glare. Also know as glass curtains.

Dormer window: An upright window which breaks the surface of a sloping roof.

Double hung: May be several items: Double-hung window, Double-hung shutters or Double-hung draperies (two sets of Draperies, usually sheer fabric under opaque fabric, both operating independently).

Drapability: How well a fabric can flow or fall into folds in an attractive manner.

Drapery: A window covering that is usually hung from a traverse rod. Draperies most often have pleated headings that may be lined or unlined.

Draw draperies: Panels of fabric, featuring pleated headings.

Dress curtains: Curtains used for the sole purpose of decorating. They are not meant to be drawn.

E

Ease: Refers to extra fabric allowance given in order to make the finished length more accurate. Sometimes fabric that was not calculated into the final length will be lost when stitching double-fold hems, headings or rod pockets, or when gathering a treatment onto a rod. It is a good idea to add ½" ease to the length before cutting to ensure a more accurate finish.

Elements of design: The elements which make up a design, including: texture, light, color, space, form, shape, pattern and ornament.

Empire: A design period dating from 1804 to 1820 in France and 1820 to 1860 in America.

End bracket: The two supporting metal grips that hold a drapery rod to the wall or ceiling. They control the amount of projection.

End housing: Refers to the box parts at the extreme ends of a traverse drapery rod. They enclose the mechanism through which the cords run.

End pleat: The final pleat in a drapery, hooked into the end bracket.

English sash window: A sliding frame consisting of a number of rectangular shaped glass panels. Also called Renaissance sash.

F

Fabric finishes: Treatments used to give the fabric more durability, decoration and usefulness. These can be chemical or mechanical.

Fabric sliding panels: Panels of fabric that are drawn with a baton. They are flat, overlapping and installed on a track rod.

Face fabric: The primary fabric on draperies or curtains. This is the fabric that faces the interior of the room.

Facing: A strip of fabric over the main fabric, with the purpose of hiding raw edges and unlined curtains or draperies.

Factory-made treatments: Custom specifications in hard window treatments ordered from a manufacturer or factory. These include shades, shutters, blinds and screens.

Fan folding: Fan folding helps to obliterate wrinkling, set the folds and provide better drapeability. This is done by folding pleated draperies into a thin band.

Fascia: A rectangular-shaped board set horizontally with the purpose of covering a curtain heading or shade fixture.

Federal Period: A design period dating from 1790 to 1820. Also called Neoclassic.

Fenestration: Location and proportion of windows in relationship to solid wall areas.

Festoon: A decorative drapery treatment of folded fabric that hangs in a graceful curve and frames the top of a window. Also called Parisian shade.

Finial: Decorative end piece on café rods or decorative traverse rods. Also referred to as pole ends.

Finished length: The length after draperies have been made, using the extra allowances in hem and heading.

Finished width: The width after draperies have been made. Found by measuring the length of the mounting board or rod and then adding in the depth of any returns.

Fixed glass: Term used to describe windows that are not made to open or close.

Flat curtain rod: A curtain rod that differs from a traverse rod in that it does not use a pulley and cord to operate.

Flemish heading: A goblet type of heading where each of the pleats are connected along their base using a hand-sewn cord.

Flounce: A technique adding an extra long heading sewn at the top of a rod pocket and having the curtain fall over the rod pocket to create the appearance of a short, attached valance.

French door draw: A swinging door or casement window with one-way traverse rods attached.

French doors: Doors in a pair, which are lengthwise, mostly made up of glass panes.

French pleats: A three-fold pleat; one of the most used pleats in draperies.

French seam: A seam most often used when the seam will be visible, or when using lightweight fabrics.

Fringe: An edging with hanging tassels or threads, used as decoration.

Fullness: The proportion of the finished width of the valance or curtain to the length of the mounting board or rod.

G

Gathered heading: A heading for a curtain or valance in which the heading is gathered by means of gathering tape.

Gathering tape: A tape stitched to the top of a curtain to create a gathered effect by pulling on cords which run through the tape.

Gathers: Folding and puckering formed when pulling on loosely-stitched thread.

Georgian Period: A design period which dates from 1700 to 1790.

Glue-baste: A technique using glue to secure two pieces of fabric together before sewing.

Goblet heading: A curtain heading having a series of handsewn tubes, in which each of the tops are stuffed with padding or contrast fabric.

Goblet pleats: Similar to pinch pleats, except that the top edge is padded and pushed out in a goblet type of shape.

Greenhouse window: A window that generally extends at a 90-degree angle from the wall, has a glass top and sides and two accompanying shelves for plants.

Group pleat: A set of pleats, generally three, with space between each one.

H

Half-canopy: A canopy above a bed in a rectangular shape, which extends only partially from the headboard down the bed.

Heading: The hemmed, usually stiffened, portion across the top of a curtain or drapery.

Hem: Refers to finished sides and bottom edges of a drapery.

Holdback: A decorative piece of hardware that holds draperies to each side of the window.

I

Insert pulley: An auxiliary traverse rod part, over which the cords operate.

Inside mount: A treatment installed inside of a window frame.

Installation: A process which undergoes the various aspects of placing and setting a window treatment.

Interlining: A fabric, usually of soft material, sewn in between the curtain and the back lining to improve bulk, insulation and overall drapability.

Inverted pleat: A pleat formed the opposite way of a traditional box pleat, in which the edges of the pleat meet in the middle right side of the fabric. Also know as the kick pleat.

J

Jabot: The decorative, vertical end of an over treatment that usually finishes a horizontal festoon.

Jalousie window: A window made from a number of horizontal slants, delivering good ventilation properties.

Jamb: Interior sides of a door or window frame.

K

Keystone arch: An arch used as part of a wooden molding for decoration, rounded and Roman in style.

Knife pleats: Narrow, finely pressed and closely spaced pleats which all go in the same direction.

L

Lambrequin: A cornice that completely frames the window. Sometimes used interchangeably with valance or cantonniere.

Laminated weights: Weight covered on both sides to avoid rust marks on draperies.

Lanai: A type of window covering made of a series of hinged, rigid plastic panels, hung from a traverse track.

Lapped seam: A seam, which is most useful for matching patterns together on the right sides of two separate pieces of fabric.

Lining: A fabric backing for a drapery.

Lintel: Wood, steel or reinforced concrete beams placed over both window and door openings to hold up the wall and roof above.

Lit a la Polonnaise: A drape set made to fall from a center point above a bed.

Lock stitch: A stitch purposely made loose, to give way for a little movement. An excellent stitch when used for holding together fabrics, linings and interlinings.

Louvers: Slats, generally made from metal, wood or plastic. These can be horizontal or vertical and are used for blinds and shutters.

M

Master carrier: Two arms that overlap in the center of a rod when draperies are closed, allowing them to close completely.

Milium: Trade name for a thermal lining.

Miniblinds: A series of one-inch, horizontal metal or plastic slats, which are held together with a cord. They can be tilted and lifted. Micro-miniblinds are similar except that the slats are only a half inch.

Miter: A technique in folding the fabric so as to keep excess fabric out of sight, eliminating bulk.

Mitered corner: The formation of the bottom edge of a drapery with a 45-degree angle on hem side.

Modern Period: A design period dating from 1900 to present.

Mullion: The vertical wood or masonry sections between a series of window frames.

Multi-draw: The simultaneous opening and closing of several draperies on one rod at one time.

Muntin: The horizontal wooden strips that separate panes of glass in windows.

N

Neoclassic Period: A design period dating from 1760 to 1789 in France, 1770 to 1820 in England and 1790 to 1820 in America.

Notch: A tiny cut, usually in a V-shape, at the edge of a fabric.

O

Off-center: A window not centered on a wall, but draperies still meet at its center point.

One-way draw: Drapery designed to draw only one way, in one panel.

Opacity: A degree measuring the amount to which solid material blocks view and light.

Open cuff: On the backside of a drapery and at top. Open cuffs make one of the strongest type headings on any drapery. This results when you carry both fabrics to the top and make a turn with the crinoline.

Oriel bay: Similar to a corbel bay window, but having the second story window descend down to the first floor.

Orientation: A term used to describe the direction in which a window faces: north, east, south or west.

Outside mount: A treatment installed over and to the side of a window frame on the wall.

Overdraperies: A layer of drapery fabric which is installed over an existing layer of drapery.

Overlap: The part of a drapery panel, which rides the master carrier of a traverse rod, and overlaps in the center when draperies are drawn closed, usually 3½" on each side.

P

Padded edge: A fabric border rolled and stuffed to form a long, round shape.

Palladian window: A window consisting of a high, rounded, middle section and two lower squared sections at each side. Also know as a Venetian window.

Panel: One half of a pair of draperies or curtains.

Passementerie: This term is used to describe the vast range of trimmings and decorative edges.

Pattern repeat: The distance between any given point in a design to where that exact point is repeated again.

Pelmet: A upholstered wood cornice or stiffened and shaped valance.

Pencil-pleat heading: Formed by a certain type of tape that, when pulled together, creates a column of tightly-packed folds.

Period window treatment: Refers to historically designed treatments from any specific design period.

Picture window: A type of window with a large center glass area with two smaller glass areas on each side.

Pinch pleats: A drapery heading where the basic pleat is divided into two or three smaller, equal pleats, sewn together at the bottom edge on the right side of the fabric.

Pin-on-hook: A metal pin to fasten draperies to a rod. It pins into drapery pleats and hooks to traverse carrier or café rod.

Piping: Cords used at the edges of a curtain for added effects, usually fabric covered and put in through a seam.

Pivot: This technique requires the machine to be stopped with the needle down in the fabric, which is turned at the corner before continuing to stitch.

Plate glass: A design which was popular in France from the Seventeenth century to the nineteenth century. Molten glass is ironed smooth after being poured onto a table, and is then made into large sheets.

Pleat: A fold of cloth sewn into place to create fullness.

Pleat to: The finished width of the fabric after it has been pleated. Example: A width of 48" fabric has been pleated to 18", i.e. "Pleat To" 18".

Pleater tape: Pocketed heading material designed to be used with pleating hooks.

Polonnaise: A bed set against the wall lengthwise, having a small, ascending dome.

Portiere: A term used to describe a doorway treatment, either a hung curtain or drapery.

Pouf shade: Shades or valances with a soft looking fabric and a gathered hem.

Pressing: An important part of sewing technique. With an iron selected to the appropriate setting for a particular fabric, a steaming method is used by lifting the iron up and pressing it down, instead of sliding it across the fabric.

Principles of design: The theory of design made possible by manipulating the elements of design to create proper balance, emphasis, proportion and scale.

Priscilla curtains: Curtains with ruffled valance, sides, bottom, hem and ties. They are usually made from sheer or opaque fabrics and sometimes they meet or cross in the center.

Projection: Refers to a jutting out, an extension. On a curtain or drapery rod, it is that part which returns to the wall from the front of the rod.

Protractor: A drapery tool by which exact angles are measured (as in bay windows).

R

Railroading: Some decorator fabrics use railroading in correspondence to widths for floor-length treatments. In this technique the lengthwise grain runs in a horizontal manner across the window treatment, making vertical seams unnecessary.

Ready-mades: Standard size draperies, factory-made and available at local stores or through mail order sources.

Renaissance Period: A design period dating from 1400 to 1600 in Italy, 1589 to 1643 in France and 1558 to 1649 in England. An era rich in art, literature, architecture and science.

Repeat: The space from one design motif to the next on a patterned fabric.

Return: The distance from the face of the rod to the wall of the casing where the bracket is attached.

Reveals: Sides to a window opening, with right angles facing the wall and window.

Rococo Period: A French design period dating from 1730 to 1760, where decorations were curved, asymmetrical and ornamental.

Rod: A metal or plastic device from which curtains are hung, an alternative to a pole. Double rods are used for two layers of fabric.

Rod pocket: A hollow sleeve in the top—and sometimes the bottom—of a curtain or drapery through which a rod is inserted. The rod is then attached to a solid wall surface.

Rod width: Measures the width between the end of a bracket to the end of the other bracket including the stackback and window width.

Roller shade: A shade operated by a device with a spring. When the spring is let loose, the shade coils itself around the device's cylinder.

Roman shade: A corded shade with rods set horizontally in back to give the shade a number of neat sideset pleats or folds when raised.

Ruching: A thin area of pleated or gathered fabric, often used for trimming or tiebacks.

Ruffle: A decorative trimming consisting of a strip of gathered fabric.

R-Value: A window treatment, ceiling or wall's capacity to keep heat in or out.

S

Sash: A wooden frame used to hold the glass of swinging and sliding windows.

Sash curtain: Any sheer material hung close to the window glass. Usually hung from spring tension rods or sash rods mounted inside the window casing.

Sash rod: A small rod, either decorative or plain, usually mounted inside a window frame on the sash.

Scalloped heading: A popular top treatment for café curtains featuring semi-circular spaces between curtain rings.

Seam: Stitching two pieces of fabric together at the right sides, leaving the stitches hidden on the other side of the fabric, for a clean, finished look on the right side.

Seam Allowance: A slim, extra allowance in the fabric between the line for stitching and the raw edge of the fabric.

Selvedge: The tightly woven edge on a width of fabric to hold the fabric together.

Shade: A window covering usually made from cloth or vinyl that covers the glass, and rolls up or down off of the window.

Shirring: A rod that is smaller than the fabric width is slid through a rod pocket to create a gathered effect in the fabric.

Shoji screen: An oriental design with paper attached to a wooden grid, forming a translucent effect with sliding or stationary panels.

Shutters: A series of folding wooden panels, which are hung by a side hinge.

Side hem: The turned part forming a finished edge at the side of the drapery.

Sill: The horizontal "ledge-like" portion of a window casing.

Skylight: A window set into a ceiling or roof, made from glass or plastic.

Slides: Small runners installed in a traverse rod which hold a drapery pin or hook.

Slip stitch: Matching colored thread is used to stitch the folded edge of a lining to the base fabric.

Smocked heading: A curtain heading consisting of a honeycomb effect. A heading full of pencil pleats hooked together at specific spacing give this effect.

Spacing: Refers to the flat space between pleats; the fuller the drapery, the less the spacing.

Spanish arch: A rounded arch designed in Spanish fashion.

Stacking: The area required for draperies when they are completely open. Also referred to as stackback.

Swag: A section of draped fabric above a window.

Tails: Shaped and stiffened or free falling, hanging trails of fabric from the end of swags.

Tambour curtains: Curtains that originally were used as folk craft in Scandinavia, they are lightweight or sheer embroidered fabrics.

Tape-gathered heading: A gathered effect for curtain headings, using thin threaded tape sewn onto the top of a curtain and then pulled by the parallel threads.

Tension Pulley: The pulley attachment through which the traverse cords move for one continuous smooth operation when a drapery is drawn. May be mounted on a baseboard, casing or wall, on one or both sides.

Tester: A canopy supported by a bed with tall corner posts.

Tie: A thin strip of fabric which is used with tiebacks to secure a drapery to a wall. The tie can be decorated or shaped.

Tiebacks: Decorative pieces of hardware, sometimes called holdbacks. Available in many forms and designed to hold draperies back from the window to allow light passage or add an additional decorative touch to the window treatment.

Tier: Curtain layers arranged one above the other with a normal overlap of 4". Upper tiers project from the wall at a greater distance than lower panels to allow each curtain to hang free.

Traverse: To draw across. A traverse drapery is one that opens or closes across a window by means of the traverse rod from which it is hung.

Traverse rod: A rod which is operated by a cord and pulley.

Turkish bed: A thin bed set back into a draped alcove.

Under-draperies: A lightweight drapery, usually a sheer, closest to the window glass. It hangs beneath a heavier over-drapery.

V

Valance: A horizontal decorative fabric treatment used at the top of draperies to screen hardware and cords.

Victorian Period: A design period dating from 1837 to 1910 in England and 1840 to 1920 in America.

W

Wall fasteners: Window treatments are fastened to hollow walls using toggle bolts or molly bolts.

Weave: The act of interlacing when forming a piece of fabric.

Weights: Lead weights are sewn into the vertical seams and corners of a drapery panel. Chain weights are small beads, strung in a line along the bottom hemline of sheers, to ensure an even hemline and straight hanging.

Width: A word to describe a single width of fabric. Several widths of fabric are sewn together to make a panel of drapery.

Zigzag stitch: One of various sewing machine settings. In this stitch, the needle moves back and forth, at the desired length and width, in a zigzag pattern. This stitch is often used for finishing seams.

A

Acetate: Used to make many persuasive artificial silks. It has similar draping and finish qualities to silk but is less likely to rot or fade.

Acrylic: A soft lightweight fabric made from a synthetic longchain polymer, primarily made of acrylonitrile.

Aluminum-coated: A lining used to help exclude light, heat and cold. It is not visible, as it faces inside the fabric, while the outside of the fabric shows woven cream cotton.

Antique satin: One of the most common drapery fabrics sold. Characterized by a lustrous effect, normally composed of rayon/acetate blends.

B

Baize: Similar to flannel and dyed green or red. Mostly used for card tables or lining silverware drawers. Its texture and color make it convenient for improvised shades or curtains. Fades in sunlight.

Basketweave: Plain under- and over-weave; primarily in draperies.

Batik: A dyeing technique developed in Java, where dye is applied and then washed, leaving bold patterns.

Batiste: A soft finished fabric, which has a high count of fine yarns. It is more opaque than voiles. Usually composed of 100% polyester or a polyester blend.

Batting: A man-made fluffy fiber, used for padding edges.

Bias: A diagonal line which intersects the crosswise and lengthwise grain of any fabric. Woven fabrics, which do not stretch at the crosswise or lengthwise grains, do stretch at the bias.

Blackout: A heavy interlining in which a layer of opaque material is placed between two pieces of cotton to block out any light. Improves the drapability qualities. It is most often white or cream.

Boucle: French for curled, indicates a curled or looped surface.

Broadcloth: (1) A medium to heavyweight twill blend or worsted wool fabric which is napped and felted. (2) A cotton fabric similar to muslin, due to its fine crosswise cords.

Brocade: Rich jacquard-woven fabric with all-over interwoven design of raised figures or flowers. Brocade has a raised surface in contrast to felt damask, and is generally made of silk, rayon and nylon yarns with or without metallic treatment.

Brocatelle: Usually made of silk or wool, similar to brocades.

Bump: Interlining imported from England, heavy weight, cotton, and available bleached or unbleached. Similar to table felt and reinforcement felt, but slightly stiffer. Cotton flannel is often used instead of bump.

Burlap: Coarse, canvas-like fabric made of jute, hemp or cotton. Also called Gunny.

C

Canvas: A heavy woven cotton and linen blend, similar to cotton duck.

Casements: Open-weave casual fabric, characterized by its instability.

Challis: One of the softest fabrics made. Normally made of rayon and sometimes combined with cotton.

Cheesecloth: Cheap and loosely woven, this fabric will easily fade, wrinkle and shrink. Similar to muslin.

Chiffon: A transparent sheer fabric with a soft finish.

Chintz: Glazed cotton fabric often printed with bright colors or large, floral designs. Some glazes will wash out in laundering. The only durable glaze is a resin finish which will withstand washing or dry cleaning. Unglazed chintz is called cretonne.

Corduroy: A cut-filling pile cloth with narrow to wide wales which run in the warp direction of the goods and made possible by the use of an extra set of filling yarns in the construction. The back is of plain or twill weave, the latter affording the better construction. Washable types are available and stretch and durable press garments of corduroy are very popular. Usually an all-cotton cloth, some corduroy is now made with nylon or rayon pile effect on a cotton backing fabric or with polyester-cotton blends.

Cotton: An inexpensive, versatile fiber which can be printed, dyed and finished in numerous ways. It also has the ability to be made colorfast and withstand light and heat. It is popular among furnishing fabrics when used alone or as a cotton blend. Its shortcomings include crushing and mildewing.

Cotton duck: A cotton varying in weight from 7 to 15 oz. per yard. Heavier types are ideal for no-sew curtains as lining is unnecessary and the edges can be glued or pinked.

Cotton lawn: Finely woven cotton, given an extremely smooth finish.

Crash: A coarse fabric having a rough, irregular surface obtained by weaving thick, uneven yarns. Usually cotton or linen, sometimes spun rayon or blends.

Cretonne: A cotton fabric usually having printed floral or angular shapes. It is a plain weave, unglazed and coarser than chintz.

Crewelwork: Indian Cotton, wool or linen fabric adorned with wool chain stitching. Most often on a cream background. Used as early American and English bed hangings.

Crinoline: A heavily-sized, stiff fabric used as a foundation to support the edge of a hem or puffed sleeve. Can be used as interlining. Also referred to as Buckram.

Crosswise grain: Crosswise grain runs perpendicular to the selvages on woven fabric.

D

Dacron: A synthetic fiber with good filling and padding qualities.

Damask: Firm, glossy jacquard-patterned fabric. Similar to brocade but flatter and reversible. Can be made from linen, cotton, rayon or silk, or a combination of fibers.

Denim: A sturdy fabric, mostly in dark blue, twill weave.

Domette: A lightweight cotton interlining imported from England. Similar to American needle-punched fleece. It is used with light shades, curtains and swags.

Dotted Swiss: A sheer fabric with opaque dots, sometimes given a raised texture.

Double knit: A fabric knitted with a double stitch on a double needle frame to provide a double thickness and is the same on both sides. Has excellent body and stability.

Dupion: Textured, real or synthetic silk. It is lightweight, which gives this fabric the tendency to rot or fade. Synthetic dupion is made from viscose and acetate and real silk dupion is typically imported from India.

E

Eyelet: Embroidered white cotton fabric often used for unlined shades or light curtains.

F

Faille: Plain weave (flat-rib); with filling yarns heavier than warp.

Figured material: A fabric whose pattern is created from the structure of the weave.

Foamback: Term used to denote that a fabric has been laminated to a backing of polyurethane foam.

Fusible buckram: A strip of white cotton filled with glue and used as a stiffener. Good for use inside of hand-pleated headings to avoid the visibility of machine stitching. It is fused to the fabric with a hot iron.

Fusible heavyweight buckram: An open-weave stiffener, made from jute and filled with glue. It is used for the base of a cornice. A hot iron will fuse it in place, releasing the glue.

G

Gauze: A sheer but coarse fabric, available in a variety of thread thicknesses.

Gimp: A wind of fabric which can be stiffened with wire or cord.

Gingham: A cheap, classic cotton fabric with a checkered pattern. The checkers come in a variety of sizes and mostly primary colors.

Glassing: Thin finish provides luster, sheen, shine or polish to some fabrics. Chintz is an example of a glazed fabric.

Grosgrain: A silk fabric with a ribbed texture on surface.

H

Hand, handle: The reaction of the sense of touch when fabrics are held in the hand. There are many factors which give "character or individuality" to a material observed through handling.

Herringbone: A versatile medium weight fabric with a zigzag pattern, named after the spine of the herring fish. It is a novelty twill weave, available mostly in neutral colors. Also called Chevron.

Holland: A linen or cotton medium-weight fabric, fade resistant and sturdy, also stiffened with oil or shellac. Standard for valances and roller shades due to its non-fraying edges.

I

Ikat: Chinese cotton or silk fabric with faint geometric patterns as a result of tie dying.

Inherent flame frees: Fabric woven of from unprocessed, flame-resistant material and flame-free for the life of the fabric.

Interfacing: A fabric stiffener used to give support and hold the shape of the fabric.

J

Jacquard: A loom which can produce woven patterns in a variety of colors. The patterns are known for being intricate and large.

Jute: An inexpensive, easily available and long lasting fabric. Comes in a neutral color but can be dyed. Like linen, it is one of the most important fabrics.

K

Khaki: A beige or earth toned, plain or twill weave fabric with a wide range of uses.

L

Lace: Openwork fabric, generally made from cotton, created by twisting and knotting threads against a net-like background to form the desired design. Lace has an endless variety of designs and is convenient for glass curtains.

Lengthwise grain: Runs parallel to the selvages on woven fabric. Fabrics are typically stronger along the lengthwise grain.

Linen: A product of the flax plant. Linen possesses rapid moisture absorption, a neutral luster and stiffness and will not soil quickly.

Linen union: A cotton-linen blend fabric, durable and reasonably priced.

M

Madras cotton: Inexpensive Indian cotton, woven in a checkered, plaid or striped fashion and brightly colored. Sometimes referred to as sari fabric.

Marquisette: An open mesh, thin fabric. Usually made from synthetic fibers.

Matelasse: Appearance of a quilted weave; figured pattern with a raised, bubbly surface.

Mesh: A term used to describe textiles or open-weave fabrics having a net-like structure.

Modacrylic: A modified fiber in which the fiber-forming substance of any long-chain synthetic polymer is composed of less than 85%, but at least 25%, acrylonitrile units.

Mohair: Comes from the Angora goat. It is lighter weight drapery fabric with a slightly brushed or hairy finish.

Moiré: A finish-given cotton, silk, acetate, rayon, nylon, etc., where bright and dim effects are observed. This is achieved by passing the fabric between engraved rollers which press the particular motif into the fabric.

Moreen: A heavyweight fabric in a wool or wool and cotton blend fabric, usually having a watered pattern.

Muslin: Usually white or off-white in color, this fabric is sheer and delicately woven, but strong.

N

Ninon: A smooth, transparent, high-textured type of voile fabric. Usually made from 100% polyester.

Non-fusible buckram: A medium-weight cotton stiffener, typically sewn into tiebacks.

Non-fusible heavyweight buckram: Two-ply double starched stiffener made from jute; unlike fusible heavyweight buckram, it is sewn onto the cornice instead of being fused. It is also easier to clean than the fusible version.

Nylon: A durable and versatile fabric, made from a long-chain polymer, originating from petroleum, air, natural gas and water. It has remarkable strength and is moderately priced.

O

Olefin: A wax-like fiber, made from petroleum products. It is lightweight but strong, and inexpensive.

Ombre: A graduate or shade effect of color used in a striped motif.

Usually ranges from light to dark tones. Also called jaspe or strie.

Organdy: Very light and thin, transparent, stiff and wiry cotton cloth. Its crispness will withstand repeated launderings Organdy is a true, durable finish cloth.

P

Padding: A soft and bulky fabric used for stuffing or filling.

Paisley: A timeless motif, this fine woolen cloth has detailed pine, floral or scroll-type designs printed or woven onto it.

Plaid: A fabric which can be printed or woven with rectangular and square shapes in a variety of colors.

Plush: A favorite of the Victorian era, this fabric is an old-fashioned form of velvet made from wool, mohair, and less often cotton, with a deeper but more thinly scattered pile. Now in modern times, it is man made.

Polyester: A stable fabric which displays excellent drapability. This fabric can be woven or knit.

Poplin: Sometimes printed decoratively, this is a plain weave with raised, circular weft cords created with large filling threads. Can be cotton, blend or synthetic and has a variety of uses.

R

Raw Edge: The edge of fabric which is cut, having neither selvage nor hem.

Rayon: Displays a texture similar to silk in touch and visibility. Rayon is available in a vast range of textures and types.

Repp: A fabric having ribbed qualities or appearance.

S

Saran: A plastic, vinyl fiber, durable and colorfast.

Sateen: A firmly woven, strong cotton or cotton blend fabric, usually having stripes or bright solid colors. The finish is smooth and shiny.

Satin weave: One of the three basic weaves, the others being plain and twill. The surface of satin weave cloth is made almost entirely of warp or filling floats since, in the repeat of the weave, each yarn of one system passes or floats over or under all but one yarn of the opposite system. Satin weaves have a host of uses including brocade, brocatelle and damask.

Selvage: Each side edge of a woven fabric and an actual part of the warp in the goods. Other names for it are listing, self edge, and raw edge.

Shantung: An inconsistently textured raw silk, once hand-woven in China's Shantung Province.

Silk: The only natural fiber that comes in a filament form, reeled from the cocoon, cultivated or wild.

Slub yarn: Yarn of any type which is irregular in diameter. May be caused by error, or may purposely be made with slubs to bring out a desired effect.

Suede cloth: A fabric made to be similar to suede leather in visibility and touch.

T

Taffeta: A fine, plain weave fabric that is smooth on both sides, usually with a sheen on its surface.

Tapestry: A heavy, well insulating fabric, once made in replication of hand-sewn tapestries, but now produced on a jacquard loom.

Tartan: A cloth fabric made of a specific checkered pattern, having particular colors of a certain Scottish clan. This fabric has great insulating qualities.

Terry cloth: This cloth fabric has uncut loops on both sides of the cloth. Terry is also made on a jacquard loom to form interesting motifs.

Texture: (1) The actual number of warp threads and filling picks per inch in any cloth that has been woven. (2) The finish and appearance of cloth.

Thread count: (1) The actual number of warp ends and filling picks per inch in a woven cloth, also known as texture. (2) In knitted fabric, thread count implies the number of wales or ribs, and the courses per inch.

Ticking: A striped cotton fabric, traditionally made of only black and white, but now comes in a wide variety of colors. It is used for covering mattresses or cushion pads, or can be made into curtains or shades.

Tricot: Usually made from nylon, this soft and thin fabric is made with crosswise elastic ribs in the back and non-elastic on top. It is seldom used for draperies due to its lack of body, but is beneficial for custom sheeting.

Tussah silk: A raw, typically Indian silk, in a yellowish-brown color, difficult to dye.

V

Velour: (1) A term loosely applied to cut pile cloths in general, but also to fabrics with a fine, raised finish. (2) A cut pile cotton fabric comparable with cotton velvet but with a greater and denser pile. (3) A stable, high-grade woolen fabric which has a close, fine, dense, erect and even nap which provides a soft, pleasing hand.

Velvet: A warp pile cloth in which a succession of rows of short cut pile stand close together so as to give an even, uniform surface. When the pile is more than one-eighth of an inch high, the cloth is usually called Plus.

Viscose (Rayon): The most ancient of man-made fibers. Well known for its distinctive sheen used in highlighting patterns and its ability to add luster and strength to cotton and silk blends.

Voile: A thin, open-mesh cloth made by a variation of plain weave. Most voiles are made of polyester. Similar to ninon, but with a much finer denier of yarn with a soft, drapable hand.

W

Warp: The yarns which run vertically or lengthwise in woven fabric.

Weft: The yarns which run horizontally in woven fabric.

Wool: An expensive versatile fabric which comes from the fleece of domesticated sheep. It has excellent insulating uses and is wrinkle and flame resistant.

Worsted: Fabric made of twisted yarn, of a wool type.

Textile Fibers & Their Properties

MAN-MADE FIBERS

Rayon

Rayon is blended with other fibers: cotton, acetate and linen.
- Drapability: good hang, soft hand
- Color fastness: good to excellent (solution dyed)
- Sun resistance: good, but not as good as cotton or linen
- Abrasion resistance: good, but not as good as cotton or nylon
- Sagging: poor, stretches in loose yarns, but OK in tightly woven fabrics
- Resiliency: good, does not pack, wrinkles less than cotton or linen
- Care: dry clean and iron at medium temperature

Acetate

Acetate blends well with other fibers, including rayon and nylon.
- Drapability: good hand, soft hand
- Color fastness: good (solution dyed)
- Sun resistance: good, but not as good as cotton or linen
- Abrasion resistance: good, but not as good as cotton or nylon
- Sagging: poor, stretches in loose yarns, but OK in tightly woven fabrics
- Resiliency: good, does not pack, wrinkles less than cotton or linen
- Care: dry clean and iron at low temperature

Polyester

Polyester is an excellent fabric for most drapery applications. It blends well with other fibers. In polyester cotton blends, the fabric will wrinkle less.
- Drapability: excellent hang, very soft hand
- Color fastness: good to excellent
- Sun resistance: excellent
- Abrasion resistance: good, sheers must be handled with care as fabric can bruise.
- Sagging: excellent, does not stretch or shrink
- Resiliency: good to excellent, does not pack, wrinkle-free
- Care: wash or dry clean and iron at low temperature

Nylon

Nylon is not widely used in drapery fabric.
- Drapability: good, soft to stiff hand, not as soft as polyesters
- Color fastness: good to excellent
- Sun resistance: poor
- Abrasion resistance: excellent
- Sagging: excellent, does not sag
- Resiliency: good to excellent, does not pack, wrinkle-free
- Care: dry clean and iron at low temperature

Acrylic

Acrylic fabrics hang well and do not sag. Can be blended with polyester. Modacrylics are flame-resistant.
- Drapability: excellent, very soft hand
- Color fastness: excellent, if solution dyed
- Sun resistance: excellent, good as cotton or linen
- Abrasion resistance: good
- Sagging: very good, does not stretch
- Resiliency: very good, does not pack, wrinkle-free
- Care: dry clean and iron at low temperature, 50 degrees

Dynel

- Drapability: excellent, soft hand like acrylic
- Color fastness: excellent
- Sun resistance: good to excellent
- Abrasion resistance: excellent
- Sagging: excellent, compared to rayon or acetate
- Resiliency: very good, does not pack, wrinkle-free,
- Low flammability
- Care: wash only, ironing does not affect it much, use low heat

NATURAL FIBERS

Cotton

Cotton generally wears excellently in drapery (print or plains).
- Drapability: excellent hang, soft hand
- Color fastness: good, vat dyes best
- Sun resistance: excellent, sun does not rot
- Abrasion resistance: excellent
- Sagging: does not stretch, except when wet
- Resiliency: poor, packs easily, wrinkles easily, very absorbent, burns
- Care: wash or dry clean and iron at high temperature

Linen or Flax

Linens are excellent in plain and casement fabric and good in prints.
- Drapability: good hang, not as soft as cotton
- Color fastness: good to poor, prints do not hold their color as well as plain fabrics
- Sun resistance: excellent, sun does not rot
- Abrasion resistance: excellent
- Sagging: strong, does not stretch
- Resiliency: poor, packs badly, does wrinkle
- Care: dry clean and iron at high temperature

Silk

Silk is rarely used in drapery today due to sun rot and cost.
- Drapability: good hang, medium to soft hand
- Color fastness: good
- Sun resistance: poor, rots in short time, lining helps
- Abrasion resistance: good
- Sagging: strong, does not sag
- Resiliency: good, does not pack badly
- Care: dry clean and iron at medium temperature

Wool

Virtually unused as drapery fabric.

Satins and Jacquards

Usually the most formal and traditional, they are generally made from tightly woven, heavy, soft material which hangs straight from top to bottom in (formal) folds.

Casements, Open Weaves

These have a lighter, more casual feel. They are usually made from loosely woven, textured yarns that hang in looser folds than the formal satins and jacquards.

Sheers

Made of soft, see-through fabrics, sheers are appropriate in most decors. Light and airy, they are sometimes used in combination with heavier draperies in more formal settings. They are billowy unless weighted, and can be made to drape quite well.

Prints

Suitable in most decors, prints are made from a light, tightly woven fabric, usually cotton or cotton-polyester blends.

Drapery Linings

Linings add substantially to the luxurious appearance necessary for good window treatments, and also provide a fuller, pleated look for maintaining a soft, drapable hand. The lined look provides uniformity to the exterior appearance of a home, while offering a broad choice of textures, weaves, colors and patterns for the interior. Linings also help to extend the life of draperies by affording some protection against the sun. They also help protect draperies from water stains—either from condensation on the inside of the window or from a sudden shower. Insulated linings contribute to energy conservation, keeping homes cooler in the summer and warmer in the winter.

Fading

The combination of sunlight and air pollution will eventually take its toll on all colors. There is no such thing as an absolutely colorfast material or dye. Some colors however will show fading more dramatically than others. Bright colors tend to show fading more than subdued tones and solids will began fading before prints.

INDEX

REFERENCES

A Portfolio of Window & Window Treatment Ideas, Creative Publishing International, 1995

Babylon, Donna, *How to Dress a Naked Window*, Krause Publications, 1997

Baker, Wendy, *The Curtain Sketchbook 2*, Randall International, 1999

Barnes, Christine, et al, *Ideas for Great Window Treatments*, Sunset Publishing Company, 2000

Beautiful Windows: Stylish Solutions from Hunter Douglas Window Fashions, Meredith Books, 2001

Cargill, Katrin, et al, *Fabrications: Over 1000 Ways to Decorate Your Home with Fabric*, Little, Brown & Company, 1999

Clark, Sally et al, *House Beautiful Windows*, Hearst Books, 1997

Clifton-Mogg, Caroline, *Curtains: A Design Source Book*, Ryland Peters & Small, 2001

Clifton-Mogg, Caroline et al, *The Curtain Book: A Sourcebook for Distinctive Curtains, Drapes, and Shades for Your Home,* Bulfinch Press, 1995

Connelly, Megan, *What's in Style: Window Treatments*, Creative Homeowner Press, 2001

Cooper, Jeremy, *Victorian and Edwardian Décor*, Abbeville Press, 1987

Cowan, Sally, *Sew a Beautiful Window:Innovative Window Treatmentsfor Every Room in the House*, Krause Publications, 2001

Creative Window Treatments (Creating Your Home), Betterway, 1996

Curtains, Creative Publishing International, 1998

Curtains for Beginners (Seams Sew Easy), Creative Publishing International, 1998

Deeds, Diane, *Arched Window Solutions*, 1stBooks Library, 2000

Durbano, Linda et al, *Two-Hour Window Treatments*, Sterling Publications, 2001

Elliott, Lynn et al, *The Smart Approach to Window Decor*, Creative Homeowner Press, 2000

Evelegh, Tessa, *Sheer Style*, Laurel Glen, 2000

Forbes, Isabella, *The Ultimate Curtain Book: A Comprehensive Guide to Creating Your Window Treatments*, Readers Digest, 2000

Gibbs, Jenny, *Curtains and Draperies: History, Design, Inspiration*, Overlook Press, 1994

Hallam, Linda, *Window Treatments*, Better Homes & Gardens Books, 1997

Harte, Negley B., *The New Draperies in the Low Countries and England*, Oxford University Press, 1998

Jenkins, Alison, *Windows: How to Make Curtains and Blinds Inspirations)*, Southwater, 2001

Lang, Donna et al, *Make It With Style:Window Shades*, Clarkson Potter, 1997

Linton, Mary Fox, Window Style: Blinds, Curtains, Screens, Shutters, Bulfinch Press, 2000

Low Sew Window Treatments (Creative Textiles), Creative Publishing International, 1997

Lowther, Richard et al, *Windows: Recipes & Ideas: Simple Solutions for the Home*, Chronicle Books, 2000

Luke, Heather, *Creative Curtainmaking Made Easy*, Watson-Guptill, 2001

Luke, Heather, *Design and Make Curtains and Drapes*, Storey Books, 1996

Martens, Claire, *Great Window Treatments*, Sterling Publications, 1998

Merrick, Catherine et al, *Encyclopedia of Curtains:Complete Curtain Maker*, Randall International, 1996

Mickey, Susan E., *Window Decor*, Sterling Publications, 2001

Miller, Judith, *Judith Miller's Guide to Period-Style Curtains and Soft Furnishings*, The Overlook Press, 2000

Miller, Judith and Martin Miller, *Victorian Style*, Mitchell Beazley, 1993

More Creative Window Treatments, Creative Publishing International, 2000

Moss, Roger W. and Gail C. Winkler, *Victorian Interior Decoration*, Henry Holt, 1992

Nielson, Karla J. and David A. Taylor, *Interiors: An Introduction*, McGraw-Hill Higher Education, 1994

Paine, Melanie, *Practical Home Decorating:Curtain and Shades*, Reader's Digest Adult, 1997

Parks, Carol, *Complete Book of Window Treatments & Curtains: Traditional & Innovative Ways to Dress Up Your Windows*, Lark Books, 1995

Simply Window Treatments, Sunset Publishing Company, 1999

Southern Living Curtains, Draperies & Shades, Sunset Publishing Company, 2000

The Editors at Eaglemoss, *Curtains, Blinds & Valances (Sew in a Weekend Series)*, Betterway, 1998

The Editors of Southern Living, *Curtains, Draperies & Shades*, Sunset Publishing Company, 2000

Thornton, Peter, *Authentic Decor: The Domestic Interior 1620-1920*, Seven Dials, 2001

Van Reenen, Lani et al, *Make Your Own Curtains& Blinds*, Storey Books, 1994

Window Dressing: From the Editors of Vogue & Butterick, Butterick Company Inc, 2000

Window Treatments (Singer Sewing Reference Library) Creative Publishing International, 1997

Windows: Beautiful Curtains, Shades, & Blinds You Can Make, Meredith Books, 2001

Windows with Style: Do-it-yourself Window Treatments, Creative Publishing International, 1997

Wingate, Isabel, *Textile Fabrics and Their Selection*, Prentice Hal, 1970

Wood, Dorothy, *Making Curtains & Blinds*, Southwater, 2001

Wrey, Caroline, *Caroline Wrey's Complete Curtain Making Course*, Overlook Press, 1997